WELFARE POLITICS IN MEXICO

The London Research Series in Geography

Geography is a wide-ranging field of knowledge, embracing all aspects of the relations between people and environments. This series makes available work of the highest quality by scholars who are, or have been, associated with the various university and polytechnic departments of geography in the London area.

One of geography's most salient characteristics is its close relationships with virtually all the sciences, arts and humanities. Drawing strength from other fields of knowledge, it also adds to their insights. This series highlights these linkages. Besides being a vehicle for advances within geography itself, the series is designed to excite the attention of the wider community of scholars and students. To this end, each volume is chosen, assessed and edited by a committee drawn from all the London colleges and the whole range of the discipline, human and physical.

WELFARE POLITICS IN MEXICO
Papering over the cracks

Peter Ward

Lecturer in Urban Geography, University of Cambridge
Fellow of Fitzwilliam College, Cambridge

London
ALLEN & UNWIN
Boston   Sydney

Allen & Unwin (Publishers) Ltd,
40 Museum Street, London WC1A 1LU, UK

Allen & Unwin (Publishers) Ltd,
Park Lane, Hemel Hempstead, Herts HP2 4TE, UK

Allen & Unwin Inc.,
8 Winchester Place, Winchester, Mass 01890, USA

Allen & Unwin (Australia) Ltd,
8 Napier Street, North Sydney, NSW 2060, Australia

First published in 1986
ISSN 0261–0485

British Library Cataloguing in Publication Data

Ward, Peter M.
    Welfare politics in Mexico: papering over the cracks.——(The London research series in geography, ISSN 0261–0485; no. 9)
1. Public welfare——Mexico
I. Title   II. Series
361'.972   HV113
ISBN 0–04–361058–7

Library of Congress Cataloging in Publication Data

Ward, Peter M., 1951–
    Welfare politics in Mexico.
(London research series in geography; 9)
Bibliography: p.
Includes indexes.
1. Public welfare—Mexico.   2. Housing policy—Mexico.
3. Public health—Mexico.   4. Mexico—Economic
conditions—1970–   .   5. Mexico—Politics and
government—1970–   .   I. Title.   II. Series.
HV113.W37   1986   361.6'0972   85–22836
ISBN 0–04–361058–7 (alk. paper)

Set in 10 on 12 point Bembo by Bedford Typesetters Ltd, Bedford,
and printed in Great Britain by Mackays of Chatham

*For Wyn, who has had enough of 'tubed water' to last a lifetime,
and for Gabriel who might never have had any.*

Preface

Are governments more likely to support social welfare provision during periods of relative economic prosperity, or during times of crisis in order to offset adverse effects of austerity measures? Mexico's recent response to this dilemma suggests that the answer is far from straightforward and may sometimes appear paradoxical. The priority accorded social welfare fell back significantly during the economic boom of the late 1970s, suggesting that full employment and rising wages made the need for social development less pressing. Once the crisis hit Mexico in 1982, social welfare programmes were pushed to the forefront and the newly elected President argued that these programmes would be given absolute priority and resources would be shifted from other sectors in order to maintain them. Although this does not appear to have occurred (social welfare's share of public expenditure continued to fall), the sector has become more effective. Peso for peso contemporary policies and programmes achieve far more than their counterparts ten years ago – hence the paradox. The devastation caused by the earthquake in September 1985 is likely to lead to a rise in resources for urban reconstruction, at least in the short term.

On page 20 of this book I suggest that some sort of reflation is inevitable given the difficulty of sustaining support from labour groups for more than a short period of austerity, and given competition from ministers seeking nomination for the next Presidential succession. Although initial indications late in 1984 and early 1985 suggested that some reflation was under way, most recent indicators suggest another recession late in 1985 extending into 1986. Major public expenditure cuts in February 1985 had been followed by a further trimming in July of 1·6% from the overall budget. Underministries are being closed and low priority investment programmes are being cancelled. Given President De la Madrid's hardnosed attitude and his apparent preparedness to sustain austerity measures far longer than many might have anticipated, the question of the succession is likely to be resolved less by how many friends can be cultivated through spreading resources around, but more by how successful ministerial candidates are at ducking the blows of expenditure cuts and responsibility for their social impact. As for overcoming social unrest, the apparently extensive ballot rigging by the PRI during the 1985 July Congressional elections, and continuing repression of the more democratic wing of the trade union movement appear to be the trade-offs that De la Madrid is willing to make in order to sustain his monetarist policies.

Continued austerity means that social welfare provision is going to play an increasingly important part in the calculus of Mexican politics. I hope that this book, complemented by the reader's own monitoring of day-to-day events, will allow an informed judgement about the role and rationale of social policy in Mexico.

PETER WARD
London, *October 1985*

Acknowledgements

The research undertaken for this book began in 1978 and spans several sources of funding. Specifically, the UK Overseas Development Administration financed the research project entitled 'Public intervention, housing and land use in Latin American cities' (PIHLU) which I co-directed with Alan Gilbert between 1978 and 1982. The British Academy supported two separate periods of fieldwork in Mexico City in 1982 and 1984. I am extremely grateful to both institutions, though I should add that responsibility for the views expressed in this book are mine alone and do not reflect those of either body.

Inevitably over a six-year period many other institutions have assisted in one form or another. The Instituto de Geografía at the National Autonomous University in Mexico City provided an office and a physical base for fieldwork in 1978–9. My period as an adviser in the Human Settlements' Ministry (SAHOP) provided a unique insight into the inner workings of government and planning in Mexico and I should like to acknowledge the support I received then and subsequently from Arq. Roberto Eibenshutz, ex-director of the Population Centres Directorate of that ministry, and now underminister of its successor SEDUE. I also thank Noemí Stolarski – a colleague and friend from that time – for her help in gathering information at various stages of the research programme. In the UK, the Department of Geography at University College London provided a supportive environment in which to work. In addition, all the computing and cartographic work has been done using Departmental facilities.

I am also indebted to an enormous number of individuals who have assisted me at some point or other with my research: not least the householders and agency personnel whom I interviewed, sometimes more than once. In particular I should like to thank Arq. Caraveo, ex-Director of Planning in the Federal District. Our many discussions always proved most illuminating and I hope that my interpretations about planning reflect creditably upon some of the major advances that his group managed to implement between 1980 and 1983. This book was written while I was in the Department of Geography at University College London, and among my colleagues at UCL I am most indebted to Alan Gilbert with whom I worked on the PIHLU project. Many of the arguments about land and servicing emerged jointly in our earlier work and I am grateful to him for allowing them to be reproduced and extended here. Two of our graduate students – Ann Varley and Sylvia Chant – have contributed directly to this book by providing comparative data for incorporation into Chapters 4 and 5. Our innumerable discussions and the fresh perspectives that they have offered are also warmly acknowledged. Bryan Roberts has spent many hours reading through various drafts of the manuscript and I am most grateful for his encouragement and perceptive comments throughout.

I am grateful to the following for granting their permission to reproduce material in this book: Dr A. G. Gilbert, *Development and Change* and Cambridge University Press.

Finally, and most of all, I should like to thank those closest to me for their support and forbearance during extended absences either abroad or in my study. To them I dedicate this book.

London, *April 1985*

Contents

List of tables

Abbreviations

AURIS	Acción Urbana e Integración Social
BANOBRAS	Banco Nacional de Obras
BNH	Banco Nacional de Habitacão (Brazil)
BNHUOPSA	Banco Nacional Hipotecaria Urbano de Obras Públicas
CANACINTRA	Cámara Nacional de la Industria de Transformación
CAVM	Comisión del Agua del Valle de México
CEAS	Comisión Estatal de Aguas y Saneamiento
CFE	Comisión de Fuerza y Electricidad
CNC	Confederación Nacional de Campesinos
CNOP	Confederación Nacional de Organizaciones Populares
CODEUR	Comisión de Desarrollo Urbano
CONAMUP	Coordinadora Nacional del Movimiento Urbano Popular
CONAPO	Comisión Nacional de Población
CONASUPO	Companía Nacional de Subsistencias Populares
CONCAMIN	Confederación de Cámaras Industriales de los Estados Unidos Mexicanos
CONCANACO	Confederación de Cámaras Nacionales de Comercio
COPARMEX	Confederación Patronal de la República Mexicana
COPEVI	Centro Operacional de Poblamiento y de Vivienda
COPLADE	Comisión de Planeación del Estado
COPLAMAR	Coordinación General del Plan Nacional de Zonas Deprimidas y Grupos Marginados
CORDIPLAN	Oficina Central de Coordinación y Planificación de la Presidencia de la República (Venezuela)
CoRett	Comisión para la Regularización de la tenencia de la tierra
COVITUR	Comisión Técnica de la Vialidad y Transporte
CRESEM	Comisión para la Regularización en el Estado de México
CTM	Confederación de Trabajadores Mexicanos
DAAC	Departamento de Asuntos Agrarios y Colonización
DART	Dirección de Areas y Recursos Territoriales (DDF)
DDF	Departamento del Distrito Federal
DDUyV	Dirección de Desarrollo Urbano y Vivienda, Estado de México
DEPROVI	Desarrollo progresivo de vivienda
DGAyS	Dirección General de Aguas y Saneamiento (DDF)
DGCP	Dirección General de Centros de Población (SAHOP)
DGCOH	Dirección General de Construcción y Operación Hidráulica (DDF)
DGHP	Dirección General de Habitación Popular (DDF)
DGOH	Dirección General de Operación Hidráulica

DIF	Desarrollo Integral de la Familia
ECLA	Economic Commission for Latin America (United Nations)
FIDEURBE	Fideicomiso de Desarrollo Urbano de la Ciudad de México
FINEZA	Fideicomiso Netzahualcóyotl
FONHAPO	Fideicomiso Fondo de Habitaciones Populares
IBRD	International Bank for Reconstruction and Development
IMF	International Monetary Fund
IMSS	Instituto Mexicano de Seguro Social
INDECO	Instituto Nacional de Desarrollo de la Comunidad
INFONAVIT	Instituto Nacional del Fondo de Vivienda para los Trabajadores
INPI	Instituto Nacional de la Protección de la Infancia
INVI	Instituto Nacional de Vivienda
ISSSTE	Instituto de Seguridad y Servicios Sociales de los Trabajadores al Servicio del Estado
MRC	Movimiento Restaurador de Colonos
OPEC	Organization of Petroleum–Exporting Countries
PAN	Partido de Acción Nacional
PARM	Partido Auténtico de la Revolución Mexicana
PCM	Partido Comunista Mexicana
PCP	Procuraduría de Colonias Populares
PDM	Partido Democrático Mexicano
PEMEX	Petróleos Mexicanos
PFV	Programa Financiero de Vivienda
PIDER	Programa de Impulso de Desarrollo Rural
PIHLU	Public Intervention, Housing and Land Use in Latin American Cities
PNR	Partido Nacional Revolucionario
PPS	Partido Popular Socialista
PRI	Partido Revolucionario Institucional
PRM	Partido de la Revolución Mexicana
PRONAL	Programa Nacional de Alimentación
PST	Partido Socialista de Trabajadores
SAM	Sistema Alimentario Mexicano
SAHOP	Secretaría de Asentamientos Humanos y Obras Públicas
SARH	Secretaría de Agricultura y Recursos Hidráulicos
SEDUE	Secretaría de Desarrollo Urbano y Ecología
SEPAFIN	Secretaría de Patrimonio y Fomento Industrial
SPP	Secretaría de Programación y Presupuesto
SRA	Secretaría de Reforma Agraria
SRH	Secretaría de Recursos Hidráulicos
SSA	Secretaría de Salubridad y Asistencia

SUDENE   Superintendency for Development in North-East Brazil
UAM   Universidad Autónoma Metropolitana
UNAM   Universidad Nacional Autónoma de México
WHO   World Health Organization

1 Economic growth and social welfare provision

State intervention in 'social issues'

Although the subtitle of this book, 'Papering over the cracks', gives some indication about the final position that I adopt it is not my intention to prejudge the role that social development plays within society. I prefer to leave the reader to decide upon the effectiveness and function of social welfare provision in Mexico in the context of the material that I present. However, the title 'Welfare politics' identifies the principal theme that I wish to analyse in some depth. Fundamentally this book is about political management. Given the complex and often contradictory functions of Latin American governments to foster economic development, control rapid population increase and urbanization, and to alleviate the worst excesses of poverty, I am interested to know more about the role of social welfare provision in the political calculus of managing those competing claims. Put simply, is social policy a sop provided by the state to keep the lid on social unrest or, viewed less cynically, is it motivated at least in part by a genuine desire to improve the quality of life of the majority of the population? And, putting motives to one side, what impact upon urban living conditions have social welfare policies had over the past 20 years? Is the picture one of general deterioration, as many writers would have us believe?

Certainly Latin American states today are, by and large, far more geared to meet the social demands placed upon them than their counterparts 30 years ago. There is a growing preparedness on the part of many governments to create institutions capable of meeting people's welfare needs. In addition, most countries have adopted a more 'technocratic' approach to problem solving so that the traditional practices of personalistic, patron–clientelism adopted by *caudillo* leaders, although not totally a thing of the past, are certainly less significant today.

In an attempt to overcome a perceived threat from so-called populist movements or from political mobilization by 'popular' sectors, some regimes have created a government structure which excludes these groups as a primary element in achieving 'order' and 'social peace' (O'Donnell 1974: 57). These are often described as 'bureaucratic authoritarian' states, typified by Brazil, Chile, Uruguay and, for much of the 1970s, Argentina. Typically they are military regimes whose administrations are highly technocratic, bureaucratic and tend to adopt a non-personalized approach to policy making (Collier 1979: 399). Where corporate structures remain, their functions are not so much those of representation but of control. However, a fundamental weakness of these regimes arises as a result of their severing links with any popular base so that they are left without adequate means to legitimize themselves. In the absence of consensus they resort to repression as a primary means of retaining power. In these circumstances, an efficient, well-managed system of social welfare provision may be an important element in keeping the populace passive. Therefore we must be careful not to misinterpret responsiveness to social welfare needs as a predisposition towards greater social justice.[1]

As we shall observe in the following chapter, Mexico does not readily comply with the classic model of 'bureaucratic authoritarianism', although state institutions are increasingly technocratic. Political pluralism exists, and there is a close (but carefully controlled) relationship between the state and popular groups. Perhaps Mexico can be best conceived as 'inclusionary authoritarian' in so far as it is not averse to using repression when absolutely necessary, but generally prefers to accommodate competing interests groups to some extent and to offer concessions to popular movements. The important point to recognize here is that the type and nature of the state determines the degree of political participation and exclusion that exists within that society; it also affects the extent to which policy making and administration is 'depoliticized' and handed over to 'technical' agencies.

The way in which the state functions is also important and a subject of considerable debate. The state itself may be best conceived as an amalgam of the government and political apparatus, the judiciary and the military (Miliband 1969). If the term 'state' is broad in the elements it embraces, its use is equally imprecise. Sometimes it refers to a general response of all constituent elements; elsewhere its use is more narrow and refers to government action. I shall use the term broadly for I am concerned here not with an attempt to sharpen past definitions, but simply to outline the alleged rationale that underpins state intervention and the functions that the state plays *vis-à-vis* different social groups. Broadly, three perspectives may be identified.[2] First, the state is sometimes viewed as a progressive entity interested in developing a form of welfare society; it engages in rational planning and spreads the benefits of economic growth to most groups in society. The state is perceived to act in the best interests of society at large, mediating between many different groups. This is now a rather outmoded view, and fails to see the state as an outcome of the class structure of society; nor does it take account of the role that the society performs in the international division of labour. The form of insertion of a given society in the world system itself conditions the structure of classes, the level of economic development and the nature of the state.

Secondly, the 'instrumentalist' perspective, most closely associated with the work of Miliband (1969, 1977), argues that the state is the tool of the dominant class in society, and acts to ensure that the interests of that class are maintained and extended. The state is manned by representatives of the dominant groups and fosters an ideology that is compatible with the interests of those groups. By contrast, the third, 'structuralist' perspective shows that the state often acts against the clearly defined interests of the dominant groups. It does this because the state responds to the structure of class conflict in ways that maintain and reproduce the conditions which favour the maintenance of the dominant groups (Poulantzas 1973). On occasions, therefore, the state is required to exercise its 'relative autonomy' from those groups in order to maintain the overall structure of domination. Unlike the 'instrumentalist' argument it is no longer necessary for the capitalist class to dominate the state apparatus physically because it controls the structure to which the state responds.

None of these perspectives is entirely satisfactory, nor are they necessarily wholly incompatible with one another (Collier 1979, Gilbert & Ward 1982, 1985). Broadly, though, the structuralist perspective best fits the Mexican case, for as we shall observe there is relatively little overlap of personnel between the governing and the economic elites. Moreover, the state has often acted against the short- and medium-term interests of dominant groups while seeking to ensure that social stability be maintained and to guarantee the reproduction of the labour force.

There is, therefore, a dilemma for the state. On the one hand it must facilitate the process of accumulation, while on the other it must make concessions to society as a whole, or to particular groups. O'Connor (1973) describes how different forms of state expenditure attempt to fulfil both the accumulation and legitimization functions. First, the state undertakes *social capital expenditures* to increase the rate of profit. These comprise social investment on projects and services that increase labour productivity (e.g. training, cheaper power and infrastructure), and social consumption expenditures which act to lower the reproduction costs of labour (e.g. 'social interest' housing, subsidies on food and public transport). Secondly, the state's legitimization function is financed by *social expense expenditures* which are not even indirectly productive but which are required to maintain social harmony or control (e.g. the provision of water standpipes, settlement improvement schemes, land regularization, vaccination campaigns). A problem arises in so far as responsibility for meeting these costs increasingly falls upon the state, yet profits continue to be appropriated privately. The growing tendency for state expenditures to increase faster than the means of financing them induces economic, social and political crises.

Castells (1979) has formulated a rather similar argument when he suggests that capitalism, faced with a declining rate of profit, requires the state to intervene increasingly to provide what he calls the 'means of collective consumption'. Essentially these comprise services that are consumed collectively (such as water and electricity). The obligation that the state provide these functions in effect politicizes the issue and provides a source of conflict around which class struggle may be mobilized. Urban groups respond to this crisis by organizing themselves into pressure groups to demand better conditions, and, as consciousness increases, this leads to social change. Given an appropriate source of conflict around which definite 'stakes' can be identified, competent political leadership may establish an urban social movement. Although there are several problems with this theory (see Saunders 1979: 118, Castells 1983, Gilbert & Ward 1985), the important point is that growing state responsibility for areas of social consumption creates a potential for political negotiation and conflict between the state and the populace. One of my main concerns in this book is to examine these political consequences in the area of social welfare provision.

The meaning of social welfare in Latin America

The term 'social welfare' is rather vague and occasionally carries pejorative overtones (Gilbert & Specht 1974, George & Wilding 1976). In the United Kingdom official statistics for the social services cover education, health, social security and local welfare services such as child care, school meals and welfare foods. Often included in this category is construction of public housing. In the USA, too, the term is used to cover similar broad areas of public expenditure (Glennerster 1975: 44). In Latin America a wide range of areas of provision may feature: social security, health, education, low-cost housing, community action, social services and basic services such as water, drainage and electricity. Although general studies about social welfare provision are rare, there are a number of specific works that analyse certain dimensions of provision such as social security (Mesa Lago 1978, Malloy 1979, Malloy & Borzutzky 1982), health care (Navarro 1974, 1978, López Acuña 1980), living standards and wage rates (Wells 1983), and housing (Hardoy & Satterthwaite 1981, Garza & Schteingart 1978).

Government statistics in Mexico record data for a 'social development sector' which includes education, health, social security, labour, human settlements and public works. Also, public federal investment by sectors identifies a 'social welfare' category for fixed capital expenditure on items such as rural and urban public works, the construction of hospitals, schools, health centres and housing.[3] Social welfare is, therefore, something of a catch-all term that may mean a variety of things in different places. For the study of Mexico I have selected certain elements for analysis: health care, water and electricity provision, and land for low-cost 'self-help' housing.

Contemporary forms and practices

Social welfare coverage in Latin America is extremely partial. A widely available free basic education programme is perhaps the exception. Since the 1950s most nations have made significant inroads in extending the network of primary education, raising literacy rates and developing secondary and higher education facilities. Although significant differences remain in the levels of service offered both between nations and between rural and urban areas, the majority of children today get some schooling and many complete at least the basic six years of primary school (World Bank 1984: 266–7).

Social security organizations which offer a comprehensive array of sickness, unemployment, retirement, accident benefits and so on are relatively rare in the continent (Mesa Lago 1978, Midgley 1984). Large organizations have been created in Brazil and Mexico, and while they offer coverage to an important proportion of the populace, their weakness is that the benefits offered are insufficient (Malloy 1979). Unemployment benefit, family benefit, subsistence allowance and so on for those who are out of work are extremely rare. Generally speaking it is the smaller organizations created to meet the needs of specific groups of workers (often in strategically important industries) that enjoy the most comprehensive benefits (Mesa Lago 1978: 6).

Neither does the equivalent of a 'national health service' exist, although most countries have a government-operated system that offers health care for those without alternative forms of coverage. In many cases the 'bottom line' is provided by charity organizations such as the Red Cross. Above this there is often a complicated heirarchy comprising different tiers of medical cover run by private enterprise, social security organizations and by the government. The quality of service provided by each system is likely to vary enormously and access is highly stratified for different social groups.

Housing provision is another area where the state has major responsibilities particularly since the early 1960s. The Alliance for Progress offered 'seed' capital to finance so-called 'social interest' housing for the majority of the population unable to afford private sector alternatives. However, sustained investment has never come close to the 1% of GNP recommended during the 'Development Decade'. The combination of weak commitment by governments and rapid rates of urbanization and population increase has meant that the rate of public sector housing production has always fallen far below demand. Invariably the units produced are too expensive for low-income groups and are acquired by better-off working-class or lower-middle income groups for whom they were, ostensibly, not designed. Once again it is the relatively privileged sectors who benefit most. The creation of worker housing banks such as the BNH in Brazil and INFONAVIT in Mexico, financed by state, workers and employers, has led to a significant increase in housing production and financing for lower-income groups during the late 1960s and early 1970s. However, although open to many more workers than previous funds, the benefits remain limited to institution affiliates and so exclude the majority.

Most people, therefore, house themselves. For the rich and well-to-do this is not a problem: they have the resources and access to credit that allows them to supervise construction of their homes according to their own designs. Or they buy ready-built dwellings from a housing developer. The poor enter the 'irregular' housing market by buying or invading land, and supervise or construct their homes through 'self-help'. Government response to such development has shifted over the past two decades. No longer is bulldozing and removal viewed as the most desirable option; instead communities are encouraged to upgrade and improve their physical environments. Services are extended to these areas and their illegal land tenancy may be 'regularized'. More recently still many countries have further embraced World Bank orthodoxy by laying out self-build settlements in the form of 'sites and services' (Payne 1984). Thus social welfare policy in the housing field now gives a little to a greater number of people, rather than relatively expensive housing units to a few. Although not without its critics, the policy has been widely accepted.

This broad review suggests, therefore, that although some form of social welfare exists, its coverage is extremely partial both spatially and socially. What, therefore, do people do when they lose their job, or fall sick and are self-employed? On a day-to-day basis how do they survive? How do they meet one-off payments such as the costs of a 'barefoot' midwife to attend the birth of their children? How can they afford to bury their dead? These may appear to be extreme examples but they are just a few of the problems that people without social welfare coverage must confront.

Traditional systems of social welfare

The strategies which poor people adopt to overcome these difficulties have been recognized implicitly for a long time but they have only recently become the subject of detailed study. Few low-income families possess sufficient savings upon which to draw in times of crisis. If hard cash is required and cannot be borrowed from friends or kin then the alternatives are the pawn shop (assuming that one has an object worth pawning), or loan sharks who charge very high rates of interest. Some households belong to an informal credit system in which an agreed sum is contributed weekly and each household takes turns to receive the pooled amount. In the event of an unexpected crisis suffered by one member, the group may allow that individual to swap their turn and take that week's savings.

Given this situation of limited savings there are four broad ways of coping which families may adopt. First, they go without. Children drop out of school (or never go in the first place) and take on some sort of employment. People stay ill: stomach complaints go uninvestigated and untreated; minor treatable illnesses become chronic. Meat, if it ever figured in the weekly diet, disappears altogether and is replaced by cheaper but less nourishing substitutes. Similarly leisure pursuits that cost money are dropped. Finally, shelter costs are minimized: some seek cheaper rental accommodation; others squat and construct dwellings made from recycled throwaways. Those who have achieved some security of land holding and have improved their dwellings to a basic level must suspend consolidation and may even lose their plots of land through failing to meet repayments.

A second strategy involves adjustments at the household level. Nuclear households may be extended by the inclusion of brothers, sisters, in-laws, married children and so on. Extended family structures offer greater security in that they are likely to have more members engaged in paid employment, so if one person loses their job there is still some income from other sources. Extended family systems also have other advantages such as mutual child care which allows more adults to work outside the home (Chant 1984). Multiple employment strategies in both nuclear and extended households frequently aim to ensure that members are represented in both the 'formal' and 'informal' sectors, thereby enjoying the benefits of both. Having at least one member in the 'formal' sector will usually ensure special health care benefits for the whole family; having others in the 'informal' sector can mean higher earning capacity. During times of wage restraint those working in the public and private sectors may suffer an erosion of purchasing power, while self-employed informal sector workers can more readily raise their prices to match inflation (Arias & Roberts 1985).

Thirdly, the poor may seek support from a wider social network that embraces kinsmen, friends and neighbours. Individual circumstances vary, of course, but these networks are often critically important sources of loans, food, child care, moral support and accommodation (Lomnitz 1977). Networks may be formalized through godparent relationships (*compadrazgo*) created around a range of events such as confirmation and graduation, not just baptisms. Occasionally, economic obligations may be so onerous that better-off families whose support is constantly sought by kinsmen are forced to remove themselves physically from the residential group in order to reduce the demands upon them (Kemper 1973).

Finally, another important source of welfare protection is patronage from one's employer. To some extent traditional relationships between workers and a patriarchical head of a family enterprise have disappeared as factories and stores get bigger and are run along corporate lines. However, many workers in small firms still go to their boss if they need financial assistance. Similarly, domestic servants and retainers frequently expect their employers to help them and their families in times of difficulty. Usually this involves a loan, cash handouts, medication and payment to visit a private doctor. Middle-class patronage of this nature is rarely analysed or taken into account. Yet it is important not only in quantitative terms in the level of protection and assistance it offers, but also ideologically and politically in so far as it reinforces dependency of one social group upon another, and sustains the continuance of discretionary patronage that pervades the social system in Latin America.

Formal expenditure on social welfare in Latin America

To what extent is social welfare or social development a priority issue for Latin American governments? I have already suggested that there is a rising expectation that the state take responsibility, but that the coverage achieved is partial and often superficial. The variability of social welfare provision expressed in terms of a percentage of total central government expenditure is displayed in Table 1.1. The data combine appropriations for education, health, welfare, social security, housing, community amenities and services, but

Table 1.1 The importance of social welfare expenditure in Central and South America.

| | GDP per capita (1982 dollars) | Percentage of total central government expenditure | | | | Percentage change social welfare 1972–1981 |
| | | Defence | | Social welfare | | |
		1972	1981	1972	1981	
Argentina	2520	8.8	11.4	35.2	42.9	+7.7
Bolivia	570	16.2	22.7	42.1	34.3	−7.8
Brazil	2240	8.3	3.4	49.2	46.0	−3.2
Chile	2210	6.1	12.0	62.3	63.4	+1.1
Colombia	1460	nd	nd	nd	nd	—
Costa Rica	1430	2.8	2.6	58.8	66.0	+7.2
Ecuador	1350	nd	11.8	nd	39.3	—
El Salvador	700	6.6	16.8	39.9	31.7	−8.2
Honduras	660	12.4	nd	41.2	nd	—
Guatemala	1130	11.0	nd	39.3	nd	—
Mexico	2270	4.2	2.5	46.6	38.9	−7.7
Nicaragua	920	12.3	11.0[a]	37.0	33.6[a]	−3.4
Panama	2120	nd	nd	.nd	38.8	—
Paraguay	1610	13.8	13.2	33.9	39.1	+5.2
Peru	1310	14.8	13.8	31.8	17.7	−14.1
Uruguay	2650	5.6	12.9	63.4	63.2	−0.2
Venezuela	4140	10.3	3.9	38.2	32.4	−5.8

Notes
[a] Figures for 1980.
Social welfare includes education, health, housing, community amenities, social security and social welfare. This incorporates central government data only and may underestimate or distort statistical portrayal of the allocation of resources, especially in those countries where lower levels of government have considerable autonomy. Includes both current and capital (development) expenditure.

Source
World Bank 1984: various tables.

because of variations in data collection and the categories used, care should be exercised in making direct comparisons between countries. However, at the level of generalization with which we are concerned the data are useful. Broadly it is apparent that in most countries social welfare is a very important element of government expenditure, usually comprising at least one-third of the total and often a much higher proportion. Defence expenditure, while often significant, is not nearly so important.[4] There is no clear trend to suggest growing or declining importance, though certain countries have experienced significant changes in one or other direction. Nor is there a clear relationship between relative levels of expenditure on social welfare and other variables such as GDP per capita or allocation for defence purposes. High social spenders include both liberal regimes, such as Costa Rica, and repressive ones, exemplified by Chile and Uruguay. Also, those that spend relatively little on social welfare include countries with both high and low rates of GDP per capita (compare Venezuela with Peru and El Salvador). Social welfare is clearly an outcome of the priorities of individual countries.

Although data are not disaggregated in Table 1.1, it is apparent that in most countries the proportion spent on education has declined, reflecting the fact that programmes of improvement in this sector were associated with the 1960s and 1970s. In contrast, most nations have sustained or developed their expenditure on health care, social security and community improvements.

Social welfare in Mexico: a declining priority?

To what extent, therefore, have Mexican governments since 1971 sought to increase the priority of social welfare provision? Traditionally the 'social development' sector has been one of the largest areas of government expenditure. Under President Echeverría (1970–76) it ran a close second to the energy sector and it was regularly a little ahead of government spending on administration and defence. Moreover, paralleling the expansion of government expenditure as a whole, in absolute terms the sector has enjoyed enormous growth from 25 billion (thousands of millions) pesos in 1970 to over 760 billion by 1982 – more than a threefold increase in real terms. Expressed thus, social development has always been an important area of government policy. But has its ranking as a government priority altered significantly in recent years?

The data suggest that the sector has lost ground, particularly under the following administration of López Portillo (1976–82). As a proportion of total expenditure, social development has declined from an average of almost 23% under Echeverría to around 18% during the following six years, with a particularly sharp fall from 1980 onwards (Table 1.2). In contrast to overall government expenditure, which increased approximately fivefold in real terms between 1970 and 1982, that of social development only tripled. A similar trend is also apparent for the López Portillo regime if one examines federal investment in non-recurrent cost items such as schools, health centres and community public works, which declined by almost 10% during the 1970s. Once again, total real investment across all sectors outstripped that of social welfare. It is clear that both the social development and social welfare sectors suffered considerable downgrading as a priority between 1976 and 1982. The sectors which received most favourable treatment were those of energy and administration (Table 1.2). The latter grew from around 20% of total government expenditure in the early 1970s to over one-half by the early 1980s – a large part of which comprised the rising public debt. The energy sector has always enjoyed a lion's share of resources and retained approximately a one-third share throughout the 1970s. Not unexpectedly, however, it felt the full brunt of the recession and declined to around 12% in the early 1980s.

Table 1.2 Public federal expenditure for different sectors including 'social development', 1972–84.

| Year | GDP in constant 1980 pesos (000 million) | Percentage of total expenditure | | | | Percentage of GDP on 'social development' |
		Administration[a]	Social development[b]	Energy[c]	Industry	
1972	2637	20 (nd)	23	28 (nd)	6	6
1974	3034	19 (8)	23	24 (13)	9	7
1976	3232	24 (8)	25	23 (13)	7	9
1978	3617	23 (14)	20	29 (18)	6	8
1980	4276	25 (17)	17	29 (19)	8	7
1982	4592	57 (46)	14	12 (9)	5	8
1983[d]	4378	55 (41)	12	13 (9)	4	6
1984[e]	nd	52 (36)	13	14 (10)	4	nd

Notes
[a] Figures in parentheses represent public debt.
[b] Between 1972 and 1976 this corresponds to education, health and social security and labour. From 1976 to 1984, labour is excluded but human settlements and public works is included.
[c] Figures in parentheses represent expenditure on PEMEX.
[d] Preliminary figure.
[e] Amount allocated in budget.

Sources
GDP figures are calculations by the author from IMF, *International Financial Statistics*, various volumes. 1972 from Jóse López Portillo. 1982 *VI Informe, anexo 1*. 1974–84 from De la Madrid. 1984 *Segundo Informe del gobierno: anexo política económica*.

Perhaps even more interesting are the data for the last two years (1983–4). The government of De la Madrid (1982–1988) has made repeated assertions to the effect that within the 'emergency programme' social development expenditure is a high priority aimed at alleviating some of the adverse social effects of the austerity measures enacted since 1982. Indeed, in his second 'State of the Nation' address (1984) the president stated publicly that the budgets of other sectors had been cut and extra resources allocated to social welfare programmes. Yet it is apparent from the actual expenditure recorded in 1983 and the budgeted allocations for 1984 that the ranking of the sector has been eroded still further (Table 1.2). There is also a decline in investment expenditure, although this is not quite so dramatic. It is certainly true that greater provision has been made for investment in housing since 1982, but this has largely come from other items of investment expenditure within the social welfare category. An increase in expenditure may now be expected over the next two to three years as the country attempts to repair the damage wrought by the 1985 earthquake.

It is clear, therefore, that the social development and social welfare sectors suffered considerable downgrading as a priority between 1970 and 1985. The important point to recognize is that although social development expenditure has increased in real terms, its overall share of resources *declined markedly*. The government has not taken the initiative to expand and develop social welfare provision as far as might have been expected given economic growth and rising government expenditure experienced during the 1970s. The strategy appears to have been one of maintaining levels of provision rather than that of development. This feature becomes apparent when one examines per capita expenditure for areas such as health and social security. They show levels of expenditure which roughly sustained the situation that existed in the early 1970s but with a sharp decline since 1982 – a point to which we return in Chapter 6.

Of course, neither a relative nor a real decline in resources necessarily implies a deterioration in social welfare services. Policies may become more efficient so that greater value for money is obtained per unit expenditure. The use of cheaper, widespread forms of preventive medicine and health care instead of expensive high-technology approaches may have a similar effect and lead to a qualitative improvement for the majority even when funding has declined. Moreover, it is important to ask who benefits? If more advantaged social groups in the past received preferential access to the benefits of social development expenditure but recent policies have tended to shift provision to the poorest, then there may have been a significant improvement in the level of provision for the majority despite a reduction in real cash funding. One cannot simply assume a deterioration because overall government resources to the sector have declined relatively or in real terms. It is necessary, also, to analyse the nature and impact of different policies of social welfare provision – the central aim of this book.

The key issues and the methodology

The main dimensions of social welfare provision examined in later chapters of this book are access to land for low-income housing, servicing poor settlements and health care. In each case my aim is to shed light on four principal questions, though the focus will not be equal between sections. First, what considerations underpin decision making by different government administrations in Mexico? Why do policies change and with what motives? Under Mexico's system of six-year non-renewable (*sexenio*) governmental regimes do left-of-centre administrations take social welfare provision more or less seriously than those in the political centre or right of centre? What determines greater or lesser government commitment?

Secondly, what are the overt and covert aims of the various bureaucracies created to handle social welfare issues? Are they becoming increasingly technical in their manner of operation and, if so, why and with what effect? Clearly agencies and bureaucracies do not operate in a political vacuum: all have political implications – even the most technically run. We need to know more about the behaviour of government bureaucracies and their outcomes.

A third issue relates to the role and importance of community mobilization, both in negotiating the receipt of the various forms of social welfare and in providing it themselves. How far are people actively involved in the struggle for social welfare provision to their settlements? Are those communities which win benefits and recognition the best organized and the most radical? Or do passive, regime-supporting settlements and groups receive greater favour? To what extent does party politics enter the calculus of political management? Also, given that there is a growing emphasis upon community self-help in government assistance programmes, we should ask who pays the economic and social costs associated with the provision or non-provision of services, housing and health care. Can the poor afford the costs imposed?

Finally, are conditions improving or getting worse? What effect has changing government commitment had upon access to social welfare, and how have living conditions changed in the past one and a half decades? How do different styles and policy priorities make for significant changes in conditions for the poor? What are the prospects for genuine improvement and what likelihood is there for significant change?

This study attempts to answer some of these questions by analysing policy and performance over three Mexican administrations: President Echeverría (1970–6), López Portillo (1976–82) and the present regime, De la Madrid (1982–8). My wish is not simply to describe the responsiveness of each administration to social issues but rather to *explain* those responses and to analyse their impact. To achieve this requires that we adopt a 'holistic' approach and I have sought to set my analysis within a broader understanding of the political economy of Mexico over the past two decades, a resumé of which is presented in the following two chapters.

Data were collected over a six-year period. This began with a year's fieldwork in Mexico City as part of a wider comparative survey of housing and servicing in three Latin American cities, of which Mexico City was one (Gilbert & Ward 1985). Various follow-up visits were made in 1982, 1983 and 1984.[5] The earlier project, 'Public intervention, housing and land use in Latin American cities' (hereafter referred to as PIHLU), attempted to collect data at a variety of levels and this methodology was sustained in subsequent visits. It combined a 'top down' view of major decision makers involved in urban development with a 'bottom up' perspective from the grassroots – in this case residents of irregular settlements that had formed illegally. I also sought to examine the linkages between the two levels as well as the ways in which high-ranking decision makers were influenced by their respective masters.

The 'top down' approach involved semi-structured interviews with those responsible for various aspects of social welfare provision. These included government ministers, agency directors, department heads, city hall administrators, politicians and so on. Although coverage was incomplete, the aim was to interview as many high ranking people as possible who had exercised influence over the areas of decision making in which we were interested (Gilbert & Ward 1985). More recent appointees who had held office since 1979 were interviewed on subsequent visits by the author. The aim at this level of survey was to gain an impression of how these individuals perceived the problem, how their policies were informed, what pressures existed to take certain lines of action, how much effective influence they wielded, and, as far as they were concerned, what influenced the specific decisions that they took? The knowledge about a particular department's past or current actions was gleaned from newspaper reports, other studies and from our direct involvement in a wide variety of settlements. It meant that I was able to delve into the decision-making process in some depth, and minimized the likelihood of the interviewee getting away with a bland answer or with empty rhetoric.

At the grassroots level, the 1978–9 survey team became involved in data collection in a number of settlements and ran a detailed household survey of over 600 families in six low-income *colonias* in Mexico City. It is not my intention to repeat here details about the manner in which those areas were selected, nor a detailed description of the survey settlements. The reader is referred to a detailed methodological statement included in the early study (Gilbert & Ward 1985: 255–70). Suffice to say that the areas were chosen to ensure comparability between them and were in the process of being upgraded and improved through self-help and community upgrading. Given that some of the findings presented in this book refer specifically to these six settlements I have included the basic data about each in the Appendix. Questions covered a range of issues and included socio-economic profiles of each family, the household structure, methods and costs of land acquisition, servicing arrangements and charges, involvement in community activities, and recent illnesses suffered by members of the household and the treatment that they received. Local leaders were also interviewed, and they provided a wealth of insight into the effectiveness of different responses to government initiatives, the most appropriate channels for state–community interaction, and how these patterns had changed over time.

The material presented in this book develops and extends much of the data that were gathered initially in 1978–9. Almost all of the household data were derived from the PIHLU settlement survey and relate to conditions in Mexico City at the end of 1978 and early 1979. I have not sought to update this data base though, where relevant, I have supplemented tables with data from other more recent surveys which adopted a similar methodology.[6] It is also important to recognize that these household data relate primarily to the capital city, so that conclusions drawn may not be directly applicable elsewhere in the country. Nevertheless, they do provide valuable insights into the opinions and behaviour of low-income residents during the late 1970s.

Elsewhere in the analysis, I have updated the research findings in subsequent fieldwork. Further interviews were undertaken both for the latter period of the López Portillo administration as well as for the most recent period under De la Madrid. Return visits were made to the settlements and contacts with the leaders renewed. Also I have sought to collect additional data at a national level to supplement the detailed earlier material gathered for Mexico City. Nevertheless, interpretations included in this study remain heavily influenced by the insights gained in the capital city. Although I believe that the processes I describe occur elsewhere, I am the first to admit that the nature of local politics may lead to substantially different outcomes. However, given that conditions are generally better in the capital, and levels of investment are disproportionately concentrated there, one may assume that the situation outside Mexico City is *worse* than that described for the city.

Notes

1   It is interesting to observe the current 'democratization' process occurring in Argentina and Brazil as both governments move from military authoritarian to democratically elected rule. Whether or not the new governments will attempt to use social welfare as a means to extend their links and control over the popular base remains to be seen.
2   This threefold categorization is an over-simplification and the actual differences between them are not so clear cut. For example, Miliband (1969) recognizes that governments do, occasionally, act against property interests or to erode some managerial prerogatives. Similarly, Poulantzas (1973: 300) does not deny that capital may exercise a strong influence over the state machinery.
3   At least up until 1982. Since that date it also has been called the 'social development' sector.
4   Although I recognise that actual expenditure upon defence may be deliberately disguised in national accounts (Ball 1984).
5   I am grateful to the British Academy for financial assistance enabling me to make return visits in 1982 and 1984. I am also indebted to my colleague Alan Gilbert for kindly agreeing to my use of the survey data collected in 1979 as part of our joint research project.
6   In particular data gathered by two doctoral students in the Department of Geography, Sylvia Chant (1984) and Ann Varley (1985) who adapted our original questionnaire to their purposes. I am grateful to them for their willingness to provide unpublished data to supplement some of my tables in this book.

2 'Boom to bust': Mexico's recent economic development

Before we can turn to analyse the politics of public welfare provision and planning it is necessary to examine the nature of Mexico's political and governmental structure. We need also to outline the recent economic changes that the country has undergone and their impact upon governmental and political life and this forms the basis of this chapter and the one which follows. In this chapter I focus attention upon Mexico's recent economic performance, and concentrate primarily upon events since the late 1960s. I examine the nature of economic structural change in recent decades and identify the objectives and outcomes of economic management since 1970. Specifically, I ask how the large body of the population has benefited from economic growth. Finally, I provide an overview of the arrangement in the capital city. Given that much of the case study material presented in this book relates primarily to Mexico City we need to know how far local structures are likely to influence the overall analysis.

The Mexican economy

Economic change prior to 1970: the years of the 'miracle'
The economic and social upheaval caused by the Revolution during the second decade of the century gave rise to one of the most stable and arguably least oppressive societies in Latin America. Yet it is also one of the most unequal. Neither rapid economic growth between 1940 and 1970 nor enormous expansion in oil production during the late 1970s has significantly changed levels of income inequality, though both processes have generated major changes in the nature of economic activity. Whether or not these changes have benefited working-class Mexicans is one of our primary concerns.

In the short term, the Revolution caused enormous disruption. Population declined; the traditional elites were overthrown and replaced by recently formed interest groups, some of which were regionally based while others were tied to different sectors of economic activity. Finally, the break-up of agricultural estates led to a period of virtual anarchy in rural areas causing production levels to fall. Except for manufacturing, which recovered quite quickly, economic performance during the 1920s and 1930s was sluggish. This was partly an outcome of worldwide depression and the decline in export earnings from precious metals, as well as inadequate foreign investment discouraged by the radical stance taken by President Cárdenas (1934–40) when he nationalized oil production and actively pursued a programme of Agrarian Reform.[1] As well as being a hero in his own time, Cárdenas laid the foundations of much of Mexico's subsequent political and economic development.

Although the development of an industrial base during the *Porfiriato* and the social and political transformations that evolved from the Revolution constitute the origins of the Mexican 'miracle', its fruition only came after 1940. Between 1940 and 1970 the Mexican economy grew at over 6% annually, and at more than 3% annually per capita. In certain sectors such as manufacturing it was significantly higher. Hansen (1974) explains this phenomenal growth as being due to several factors. First, political stability was achieved during the 1930s and institutionalized in a single governing party (the PRI – discussed in Chapter 3). Secondly, public financial institutions such as the Banco de México and Nacional Financiera became the vehicles for large-scale state support and intervention in economic development. In the early period (1940–50) these institutions underwrote the development of basic industries, while later they directed investment to infrastructure such as electric power and railways. Other state interventions were also important and helped stimulate rural to urban migration – necessary to supply adequate cheap labour to the cities. Thirdly, changes in the social and psychological make-up of the elite and the new opportunities for socio-economic mobility enhanced development (Hansen 1974).

How extensive was this development? In agriculture, production rates grew very fast at the outset, but dropped back to average 4.3% between 1950 and 1960 and 2% in the last five years of the 1960s (Scott 1982: 77). By 1970 there were clear indications that agricultural production was in crisis. The production of certain staples was falling behind demand, guaranteed prices for basic foodstuffs had declined in real terms and land was increasingly being turned over to export crops and to cattle rearing (Tello 1978: 15–22, Heath 1985). However, the state response was ineffective as much of the assistance and the new techniques associated with the 'Green Revolution' favoured the larger, more commercialized farming units (Cockcroft 1983: 165–73). Increased production levels were especially marked in the highly capitalized sectors of sugar, coffee, market gardening and cotton. Cotton alone contributed 18% of commodity earnings abroad. Yet despite the pressures working against them, small-scale peasant farmers still generated 40% of the corn crop. Indeed, overall production on *ejidos* (lands distributed to peasants as part of the Agrarian Reform) kept pace with that on private farms though the former concentrated much more on the production of staples (Hansen 1974). Nevertheless, the overall effect of agricultural development between 1950 and 1970 was to reduce the opportunities and viability of the smallholder. Between 1950 and 1960 the level of landlessness rose from 2.3 million to 3.3 million (Hansen 1974: 81), and the proportion of the total labour force employed in agriculture declined from 65% in 1940 to 39% by 1970 (Table 2.1). Similarly its share of GDP declined from 23% in 1950, to 16% in 1960 and to 11% in 1970 (United Nations 1980).

It was in industrial development that the 'miracle' was most pronounced.

Table 2.1 Economically active population by sector, 1940–79 (percentages).

	1940	1960	1970	1979
total workforce (millions)	5.86	11.27	13.18	19.7
agriculture	65	54	39	29
industry	15	19	22	28
mining/petroleum	2	1	1	1
manufacturing	11	14	17	20
construction	2	4	4	6
electricity	0.4	0.4	0.4	0.7
services	19	27	32	43
commerce	8	10	9	14
transport, etc.	3	3	3	3
other	9	13	20	26
not specified	—	1	6	1

Sources
Cockcroft (1983: 183). Unfortunately since 1979 neither the SPP *Encuesta continua sobre la ocupación*, nor the government *Informes* give data about the percentage employed in different activities. The SPP gives quarterly data for the three major metropolitan areas based upon a sample survey. This has become a very sensitive political issue since 1982.

Manufacturing grew at over 8% annually (Hansen 1974: 41). Import-substituting industrialization complemented investment in activities that produced goods for export. The state intervened to enhance Mexican competitiveness abroad by devaluing the peso in 1949 and 1954 and by holding down wage increases. Foreign investment in Mexican industries was stimulated by providing infrastructure, tax incentives for new firms, low rates of tax generally, and special concessions in the US–Mexican border zone which made it highly profitable for US companies to establish industries in that area using Mexican labour.

This very successful period of economic growth had widespread repercussions upon both the total population and its distribution. Total population increased rapidly from 19.6 million in 1940 to an estimated 73 million in 1982 (IMF 1984: 314). Also, Mexico became primarily an urban country. The proportion of the national population living in urban areas (defined as more than 10 000 people) rose from 22% in 1940 to 42.3% in 1970, and in the early 1980s stood at around 55% (Scott 1982: 53).

Yet despite the impressive rates of economic growth recorded, the distribution of incomes has not altered significantly. Indeed, it appears that the early phase of rapid economic growth was achieved at the expense of growing income inequality. Measures of inequality show an increase during the 1950s when the position of the poorest income groups deteriorated (Makin 1984). In the 1960s the lowest 40% of the economically active population earned only 11% of the national income, and there were pessimistic forecasts that this situation was unlikely to alter appreciably during the 1970s (Navarette 1970). In fact some recent progress has been made. The level of income inequality has declined (from a Gini coefficient of 0.551 in 1956 to 0.503 in 1977; Makin 1984: Table 2.6). With the single exception of the lowest paid 10%, all income groups have improved their position in absolute terms. But, if the fruits of economic growth have trickled down to a limited extent, they have fallen mostly into the laps of the middle and upper-middle income groups. The Mexican 'miracle' appears to have resulted in a redistribution of incomes in favour of these middle income groups at the expense of the top and bottom sectors (Hansen 1974). Income distribution of Mexico remains one of the most unequal of all Latin American nations (Weisskoff & Figueroa 1976).

Also, by 1970 the high social costs associated with economic development were beginning to surface. Wage levels and employment conditions were worsening and the 1970 census revealed enormous levels of deprivation among large sectors of the population. There were also political consequences: growing alienation among the intelligentsia; increasing unrest in rural areas and the first signs of groundswell of public protest in low-income areas of the cities. In particular the disturbances of 1968 and 1971 were key signals which demanded adjustment to the policies that had previously sustained the so-called period of 'stable development' and heralded a period that was, perhaps optimistically, referred to as 'shared development'.

'Boom and bust': economic instability since 1970

ECONOMIC MANAGEMENT AND CRISES, 1970-84   In order to tackle some of these problems, incoming president Echeverría sought to assert the directive role of the state in the national economy and created or revitalized a large number of state enterprises in the fields of production, distribution and welfare (Tello 1978, Needler 1982, Goulet 1983). Public sector expenditure in social welfare increased significantly in real terms. Wages were increased and tax reforms proposed, as were other actions which sought to favour the working classes at the expense of the private sector (Tello 1978). Inevitably many of these proposals encountered strong resistance from elite groups (Cockcroft 1983), but they failed, ultimately, not because of that opposition but rather as a result of a combination of national and international factors. The promise of gradual structural changes to the economy foundered, and the period emerged as one of disequilibrium and erratic economic expansion.

Although the overall economy continued to grow at a satisfactory rate during the 1970s (at an average of 5.9% of GDP between 1971 and 1980) it has not been a smooth passage (Padilla Aragón 1981: 14). Whereas between 1963 and 1970 the growth of GDP per annum never fell below 6.3%, the period 1971 to 1980 saw it fall below 6% on several occasions (Table 2.2). Three 'depressions' figure prominently: the first began late in the administration of Díaz Ordaz and

Table 2.2 Growth, prices and purchasing power, 1960–83.

Year	Percentage increase GDP over previous year	Percentage GDP per capita (rate of development)	Inflation: percentage increase in consumer price index	Purchasing power over previous year: percentage variation	
				Minimum salary	Wages in manufacturing industry
1970	6.9	3.5	7.0	10.8	2.7
1971	3.5	0.1	5.3	−5.1	−0.1
1972	7.9	5.0	5.0	12.6	0.5
1973	8.2	4.9	12.0	−6.2	−5.2
1974	6.3	2.8	23.8	9.9	−4.5
1975	3.0	2.4	15.2	0.9	1.2
1976	2.1	1.2	15.8	11.6	0.7
1977	3.4	0.5	28.9	−0.9	−0.8
1978	8.3	5.2	17.5	−3.4	−2.9
1979	9.2	6.2	18.2	−1.1	−1.1
1980	8.3	5.4	26.3	−6.6	−3.7
1981	7.9	5.1	28.5	2.3	1.9
1982	−0.6	−3.1	57.6	−1.9	−3.3
1983	−4.7	nd	102.7	nd	nd

Sources
Column 1: GDP figures are calculations by the author based upon IMF, *International financial statistics*, various volumes. 1984 projection *El Financiero*, 4 October 1984.
Column 2: *Indicadores económicos 1965–1982*, Banco de México, August 1984.
Columns 3 and 4: Banco de México, *Cuaderno mensual, Indices de precios*, 75, July 1984. Consumer price index, calculations by author. Percentages show price rise over previous year.

reached its worst point in 1971; the second began in 1973 but its impact did not really become discernible until the latter part of 1974 and culminated in a near 100% devaluation of the peso just before Echeverría left office in 1976. The economy did not pick up again until López Portillo reflated in 1978 and thereby abandoned policies imposed by the IMF as conditions for its support. Unfortunately, the spurt of economic development in the late 1970s was short lived and failed to touch, in any appreciable way, the underlying structure that had contributed to the earlier crisis. A third 'depression' emerged as the economy overheated, bringing about further devaluations and IMF intervention in 1982–3. During each crisis the GDP growth rate per capita dipped below 1% (Table 2.2).

These crises are partly an outcome of the Mexican system of mandatory change of government every six years and reflect a degree of heady largesse in matters of public policy during the final months of one administration. They are also an outcome of demands by the president-elect that the incumbent 'clean the slate' and carry out any measures that are likely to be unpopular (such as devaluation) before the new Executive takes over. This was a feature of the handover in both 1976 and 1982. Indeed some authors view this regular renewal as a positive advantage, allowing a clean break to be made and new commitments to be forged (Whitehead 1980, Purcell & Purcell 1980). When López Portillo took office he was able to appear as conciliator between the government and the private sector, and the simple fact of his accession did much to restore public confidence.

A recent view, with which I concur, is that all presidents are committed to economic expansion from their fourth year onwards if not before (Whitehead 1984). Policies of economic austerity oblige the state to make deals with those social groups that are likely to suffer most and upon which, ultimately, they depend for their legitimacy (e.g. the unions and the poor), but such agreements can only be expected to endure for two or three years, after which growing unrest demands some degree of reflation. Also, inter-ministerial competition associated with the struggle to win the nomination for the presidential succession creates strong spending pressures which the incumbent is unable to prevent totally. Indeed, in 1984 there were already signs of growing unrest and of unwillingness on the part of the trade unions to continue to co-operate. It is also evident that some degree of reflation is underway. However, given the intensity of the current crisis and the difficulty of discerning where the money might come from for reflation, President De la Madrid may be more successful than his predecessors at applying the brake, at least for the greater part of his administration (*Proceso*, 10 September 1984).

But it would be wrong to suggest that these crises are merely a sexennial phenomenon: external and internal factors are also important. The international recession and rising prices from 1973 onwards, a growing balance of payments deficit, inflation and the transfer of capital out of the country were important factors which contributed to undermine the economic strategy of the Echeverría administration. Similarly the effects of inflation, overextended public sector expenditure, and a growing balance of payments deficit (partly induced by the enormous purchases of foreign technology for the exploitation of oil resources and for industrialization) led to spiralling indebtedness from 1978 onwards. When at the end of 1981 Mexico was obliged to cut the price of its oil by eight dollars a barrel in line with other oil producing countries, the country found itself broke. In effect the depressed price of oil meant a loss of ten billion dollars in earnings during the first half of 1982 (Cockcroft 1983: 269). Much of this anticipated revenue had already been earmarked and spent.

In part these crises reflect mismanagement, corrupt practices and bad luck. Inevitably, also, they are a consequence of the relationship with the USA and with other developed nations. The Mexican economy is not its own. Despite a 'Mexicanization' law which is supposed to ensure that a majority of stock remains in the hands of Mexican nationals, much of the investment comes from outside and often constitutes a controlling interest. Indeed, in certain areas of economic activity regarded as 'non-strategic', this law no longer applies. The ratio of profits leaving the country through multinational corporations against new investments is very high, and leads to an overall 'decapitalization' and 'dollarization' of the economy (Cockcroft 1983: 256). Many of the larger industrial enterprises are dominated directly or indirectly by the multinationals; basic foodstuffs have to be imported (despite attempts by the SAM and more recently PRONAL to encourage self-sufficiency), and imported goods far outweigh revenues from exports, even taking into account the greatly increased revenues derived from petroleum. Finally, the most important sources of credit originate abroad.[2] In 1982 the costs of debt servicing alone amounted to over one-half of the revenues derived from exports.

The deepening nature of this dependency relationship invariably works to the advantage of the external power, not simply in terms of growing access to a cheaper workforce that can be readily hired and fired according to the dictates of the originating economy, but also in the influence that can be exercised by the dominant power in negotiations in the area of foreign policy, and for the purchase of commodities such as oil, natural gas and technology. There is considerable evidence that, in exchange for credit, Mexico has been forced to provide the USA with greater quantities of oil and gas than it would have wished, and at prices preferential to the latter (Cockcroft 1983: 270).

Since 1983 Mexico has struggled to work its way out of the economic crisis, and while showing considerable success has found high US interest rates an unanticipated extra burden. Public spending has been cut, as has expenditure on imports, particularly in the area of capital goods which were reduced by 60% (in value) in 1983 (Comercio Exterior, April 1984: 360). Attempts have been made to encourage foreign investment. Inflation in 1983 was reduced to 81% (still very high but no mean achievement given the 100% inflation recorded in 1982 and the runaway trend of the first few months of 1983), and came down to around 59% in 1984 (though the target was 40%). Wage rises have been severely restrained: in 1983 their real value was eroded by an estimated 23% and was pegged to accommodate inflation in 1984 (Table 2.2). Debts amounting to 23 billion dollars that were due to be repaid between August 1982 and December 1984 have been successfully rescheduled to provide four years' grace with repayments spread over a further four years (Comercio Exterior, April 1984: 364). Longer-term rescheduling has also been negotiated which effectively shifts the burden of repayment into the following two sexenios. However, the peso again threatens to become overvalued and was again devalued by 30% in July 1985. If one accepts the earlier argument concerning the inevitability of reflation, then the question really becomes one of when: 1985 or 1986? At the beginning of 1985 it looked as if some reflation was underway.[3] Certainly there were signs that the Government was unwilling to keep strictly to the conditions set by the IMF. However, cuts in oil prices and a slump in trade has forced further austerity measures in February and July 1985. Reflation, if it happens, has been postponed for a year.

SECTORAL PERFORMANCE, 1970-84   Since 1970 the several sectors of the economy have been affected in different ways. In terms of contribution to GDP and relative importance as an employer of the economically active population, agriculture has fared particularly badly, although its decline began much earlier than the 1970 cut-off point considered here. The industrial sector, and in particular manufacturing, has grown sharply both in terms of its contribution to GDP (from 31% for industry in 1965 to 40% by 1983), as well as in employment opportunities that have been created. In recent years, of course, petroleum has reinforced the contribution that this sector makes to GDP, though it generates relatively few jobs. Services and commerce have always been important, and since the 1960s have contributed over 50% of GDP. However, its significance in absorbing labour has increased dramatically over the same period: from 27% of the economically active population in 1960 to over 43% by the early 1980s (Table 2.1). Much of the growth observed in services has involved the creation of 'genuine' jobs in banking, large-scale commerce and so on. However, it also includes the atomization of jobs within the tertiary sector – in activities such as small family businesses, individual stalls, lottery ticket sales and so on.

In manufacturing there has been a significant shift in emphasis and a concerted effort to move away from the United Nations ECLA-inspired models of import-substituting industrialization which, it was widely recognized, had failed to generate sufficient jobs and was leading to an increase in dependence upon imported technology, capital and raw materials. Instead, investment has focused upon industries which utilize locally occurring natural resources – such as food processing, mining, and petroleum production and petrochemicals (Needler 1982: 100). An attempt was also made to extend 'backward' industrial linkages by developing machine tools and the production of other capital goods, themselves often dependent upon steel. However, at least in the short term, this process has threatened to increase Mexican dependence, given that much of the 'seed' technology is developed outside the country (Cockcroft 1983: 256). According to one source there was a ninefold increase in production goods imports during the 1970s which led to the dramatic rise in the public sector debt (*ibid.*: 256).

The important point to recognize here is that while overall economic expansion occurred during the 1970s, it has been a stop–start process and was mainly concentrated within the industrial sector. While this generated consider-able employment, particularly in manufacturing, the largest growth area as far as jobs are concerned has been in the service sector. The expansion of the public bureaucracy during the 1960s and especially in the 1970s was another important feature of the changing structure throughout the period. Inevitably these processes have had major repercussions upon the prospects for employment and wage levels – points to which I return below.

THE IMPACT OF OIL PRODUCTION   Within this sharply contrasting economic performance oil has been both a boon and a bane. While the rapid rise in known reserves and the dramatic increase in production allowed López Portillo to reflate the economy, it also led ultimately to economic collapse. Knowledge about the extent of known reserves was a carefully guarded secret from 1974 onwards.[4] At the end of the Echeverría period reserves were set at 6 billion barrels; López Portillo raised this estimate in 1978 to 20 billion, and again in 1979 to 40 billion (Whitehead 1980). In 1982 Mexico's reserves were set at 72 billion barrels and an eventual level of 250 billion barrels is not beyond the bounds of possibility. This would place Mexico not far behind Saudi Arabia in the oil-producing league (Cockcroft 1983: 261).

At the outset of the boom in petroleum production the government expressed its firm intention to avoid squandering revenues from oil. It did not wish to encourage consumption of expensive consumer durables, nor was it prepared to bail out the purchase of food imports on a continuing basis. In the rhetoric of the day, oil was a national patrimony to be shared by all and to be used to generate long-term development. Moreover, no single country was to receive more than 50% of total exports in an attempt to avoid the dangers associated with over-dependence on a single source of foreign earnings. As a consequence a daily production limit of 1.5 million barrels was set throughout the 1980s (Cockcroft 1983: 262). Yet this was later raised to 2.2 million barrels and production at the end of 1982 was scheduled to reach 2.7 million (Needler 1982: 109). Works to expand port development to cope with much higher levels of oil production also suggested that in the future these production ceilings would count for little. Moreover, despite the guideline about a maximum level of exports to any single country, by 1981 more than four-fifths was going to the USA. The crux of the problem was that Mexico needed the money: the only way out of the spiralling indebtedness was to increase oil production. Also important, however, was external pressure from the USA to provide increasing amounts of oil and gas for its consumption, thereby allowing that country to conserve the rate at which it was obliged to exploit its own reserves. The substance of that pressure was the threat to withhold financial credit.

Oil production also fuelled the crisis in another way. Inevitably, perhaps, almost all of the technology required to extract the resource had to be purchased from abroad. This meant that PEMEX, the state oil company, was spending much of its revenue. By mid-1982 it had accumulated a foreign debt of 25 billion dollars – one-third of the nation's total (see Whitehead 1980, Cockcroft 1983: 262).

THE PROBLEM OF INDEBTEDNESS   The absolute size of the public debt has grown inexorably since the mid-1970s and accounted for a large slice of public expenditure by 1982 (Table 1.2). This rise reflects the growth of new credits, the effect of devaluations and, more recently, high interest rates in the USA. By 1984 Mexico's foreign debt totalled 89 billion dollars which, along with Brazil, was the developing world's highest. More immediately the problem is one of servicing the debt, and when in 1983 De la Madrid announced that Mexico was going to find it difficult to meet even the interest payments, further interim credits were provided. Since then a large proportion of debt repayment has been rescheduled. Under López Portillo, from 1978 onwards interest and debt repayments consumed over one-half of foreign exchange earnings (Padilla Aragón 1981: 36). In 1984 this ratio had been reduced to 24% (*The Sunday Times*, 13 May 1984).

Some attempt has been made to raise revenues through taxation. Echeverría initiated higher rates of income tax and raised the efficiency with which they were collected. However, the relative contribution made by income tax compared to other forms of tax (oil, imports etc.) fell from 51% to 33% between 1979 and 1981 (Padilla Aragón 1981: 53). Moreover, López Portillo raised the thresholds upon which income tax was liable, and imposed value-added taxes so that the net effect of tax reform under his administration was to produce a more regressive structure (Needler 1982: 108). Since taking office his successor has increased further the rates of value-added tax and extended them to all but basic subsistence commodities.

The benefits of growth: employment and wages
The pattern of growth and contraction that I have described had an important impact upon access to employment, the opportunities for economic mobility and the value of real wages. But as we have observed this period also saw a shift in the structure of the Mexican economy, particularly in relation to the nature and scale of activities carried out within the industrial and service sectors. The imposition of austerity measures by the IMF seriously affected government expenditure and wage levels. The changing nature of employment and wages, therefore, were a response to all of these factors and are not simply an outcome of the rate of economic expansion. The important question to ask here is whether the poor benefited significantly from the changes introduced since 1970 and from the oil bonanza?

For several reasons the broad answer to this question is no. The Mexican workforce is increasingly vulnerable to international economic changes. The level of labour utilization in Mexico is low compared with most other Latin American countries (around 27% of the population), and has actually declined from 39% at the beginning of the century. According to some authors this suits capital in so far as it represents a 'reserve army' of labour that may be maintained without cost and absorbed when required, as well as functioning to keep wage levels low, to weaken attempts at labour mobilization for improved conditions, etc. (Cockcroft 1983, but cf. Roberts 1978). Labour can be regularly hired and fired according to the amount of work available, or to ensure passivity of the workforce, or to avoid contractual obligations required for 'permanent' employees. They are also arguably 'superexploited' not simply by being paid low wages but by increasing intensity of work and by extension to the working day (Cockcroft 1983: 221). Vulnerability is further heightened by the growing use of capital-intensive technology in industry, which generates less employment per unit cost investment – arguably an undesirable trend given Mexico's youthful age structure, and the estimated 800 000 new jobs required each year to allow for those entering the labour market for the first time and the growing participation of women in the economy (Mexico SPP 1983b: 215).

Vulnerability also arises from the fact that so much recent industrial investment comes from outside the country. Increasingly we may conceive of an international division of labour whereby transnational companies utilize the relatively cheap labour available in Mexico and effectively decide the workforce's livelihood. This is not a feature unique to Mexico alone: it is a familiar enough problem in the UK. But Mexican workers are more vulnerable than their British counterparts because the level of dependence upon external companies is greater and because their activities are often limited entirely to the assembly of imported goods. There is considerable truth in the maxim that when the USA sneezes, Mexico catches cold.

UNEMPLOYMENT Unemployment has shown a clear tendency to increase during the periods of economic depression identified earlier. In both 1974–5 and 1982 many factories were closed down temporarily and others went bust, as did many small-scale businesses. There are few good data available that describe unemployment or underemployment at a national level, although one estimate suggests that early in 1975 more than four million workers were affected (amounting to 25% of the economically active population; Padilla Aragón 1981: 32). It is estimated that in 1984 approximately two in every five Mexicans did not have full-time employment. Between 1981 and 1983 the rate of 'urban unemployment' nationally rose from 4.2% to 12.5%.[5]

There is some evidence to suggest that families today are consciously adopting a 'strategy' to maximize their employment opportunities. In rural areas it has been argued that many peasants have become 'proletarianized' and now work as wage labour on large-scale commercial farms, while at the same time they utilize family labour in subsistence farming or in handicrafts in order to survive economically (Cockcroft 1983: 89). Multiple-earning strategies have long been utilized in the *maquiladora* industries in the north which employ a large female workforce. (*Maquiladora* industries are those which assemble and 'finish off' goods that are imported from the USA 'in-bond', for return to the United States as finished products.) There are suggestions that similar patterns may be observed elsewhere and that they may have growing relevance for urban areas (Pommier 1982: 352, Cockcroft 1983: 222).

Neither should we assume that given a choice people automatically opt for employment in the 'formal' sector – an industrial job, for example. Recent labour market studies in Guadalajara, which has a tradition of 'outwork' in clothing and shoemaking, suggest that some self-employment or employment in the 'informal sector' may maximize the household's earning power (Arias & Roberts 1985). Also, as we observed in Chapter 1, during periods of wage restraint informal sector activities are not subject to the same restrictions as formal employment: prices and fees can be raised more readily to meet inflation. Although it might be sensible to have one household member employed in an industrial enterprise, thereby enabling the family to qualify for social security, it may be economically and socially more convenient to work 'casually'.

Nevertheless, it does appear that during times of crisis when workers are shed from the industrial sector they seek employment in the tertiary sector. Indeed, if they are to work at all there is no other alternative. In Mexico City, for example, tertiary sector employment expanded between 1974 and 1978, and this cannot totally be explained by an expansion of civil service jobs (Pommier 1982).

INFLATION AND WAGES   The whole of this period is epitomized by rapid inflation. Between 1971 and 1978 it averaged 15.2% annually in contrast with 2.8% between 1959 and 1970 (Padilla Aragón 1981: 20). Since 1977 it has spiralled to 25% per annum (1977–80) and to almost 100% in 1982 and 1983. It declined in 1984 but overshot the 40% target for that year. Wages have not increased concomitantly. Although real wage levels were restored in 1974 to above their previous highest level, the purchasing power declined sharply after 1977 (Table 2.2; see also Bortz 1983: 103). Maximum wage increments (*topes*) allowed for workers were negotiated by the government and the unions between 1977 and 1980 and again in 1983, but these fell far below price increases over the same period.

In Mexico the traditional means of protecting the value of real wages has been one of regular (usually annual) revision of the daily minimum wage. In times of rapid inflation or after a devaluation, minimum wages have been renegotiated but have usually resulted in an erosion of purchasing power. They take a month or two to introduce, while in contrast prices are raised overnight, bringing about short-term hardship. Since late 1982 there has been some call from organized labour for the introduction of a 'sliding scale' whereby wages are automatically adjusted every three months to take account of price increases (Bortz 1983, Garavita Elias 1983). During the early months of 1983 the government was lukewarm in its response to the idea. Although it was never admitted publicly, a sliding scale adjusted automatically every three months would have reduced the bargaining strength of the government in its relations with labour. Also, from the government point of view faced with appeasing the IMF, a decline in real wages was both anti-inflationary and provided a windfall to capital whose production costs were thereby reduced. Nevertheless, as a concession to the unions, the Ministry of Labour agreed to allow the Minimum Salaries' Commission to meet 'as often as required'.

Therefore, in terms of changing access to employment opportunities, levels of full employment for both men and women and the value of real wages, the impact of economic growth upon the wellbeing of the average Mexican worker has been extremely limited. Granted, during the buoyant periods employment has expanded, but there has been little evidence of fundamental structural changes that will enhance future employment prospects. Quite the opposite: the industrial structure has become more dependent upon foreign technology and capital; it has become more capital intensive; and the level of indebtedness means that any freedom to manoeuvre that the government might have exercised will be severely curtailed. The first round in the battle to use oil resources to guarantee the country's future has been resoundingly lost.

Economy and urbanization in Mexico City

Much of the case study material analysed in this book relates primarily to Mexico City. Therefore it is necessary to describe briefly the demography, economy and government of the city. In particular we may question the degree to which Mexico City – the national capital – receives preferential treatment compared with other areas of the country. If it does then we must assume that conditions elsewhere may be considerably worse than those described by much of the data presented in this book.

Political boundaries and urban growth

The Federal District is divided into 16 *delegaciones* or sub-mayoralties, three of which (Milpa Alta, Tlahuac and Cuajimalpa in the south) remain largely unurbanized (Fig. 2.1). Much of the early city growth until 1940 was concentrated within the central area which now constitutes four *delegaciónes*. Thereafter, rapid urbanization and suburbanization extended into surrounding *delegaciones* in the north, east and south-east. Finally, in the late 1950s and early 1960s, development spilled over into the State of Mexico. This process was stimulated by the sale of cheap plots of land for the poor, and by the growth of job opportunities associated with new industrial enterprises that were encouraged to locate on the other side of the Federal District boundary.

The pace of much of this urbanization was extremely rapid. Municipalities such as Netzahualcóyotl in the east, which were not even formally constituted in 1960, possessed 700 000 residents a decade later. The vast majority of these people were poor. By 1970 the city population numbered 8.5 million, 19% of whom lived outside the Federal District. This has since increased to 13.2 million by 1980, 33% of whom live in the surrounding municipalities. In 1980 Netzahualcóyotl had an estimated 1.5 million people living within its boundaries. The limits of the Federal District, surrounding municipalities and the built-up area are shown in Figure 2.1.

During the earlier phase of urbanization (pre-1940), migration to the city fuelled this growth. However, the youthful age structure of the city and high rates of natural increase have meant that the largest share of subsequent growth comprises people born in the city. Migrants continue to arrive in increasing numbers, but their relative contribution to city growth is now of secondary importance to natural increase.

Figure 2.1 Political boundaries and built-up area of Mexico City.

Mexico City: a privileged citizenry

Compared with the rest of the country Mexico City is privileged in several respects. In economic terms it enjoys a disproportionate share of GNP. In 1970 the city's share of total GDP was 37%; yet it contained only 18% of the total population. In 1979 and 1980 the Federal District received 58% and 54% of all private investment in the country (Makin 1984: 73).

The urban economy changed little between 1960 and 1970. Around 31% of the economically active population were employed in manufacturing, though data for gross internal product show a substantial decline in the contribution made by this sector (Garza 1978: 35). Those engaged in services rose from 33%

to 37%, but employment in commerce and finance declined substantially (from 17.3% to 13.7%).

During the 1970s changes reflect closely the national economic fortunes described earlier. Within the Federal District the cycles of unemployment associated with economic decline are quite clearly enunciated (Pommier 1982). Unemployment reached its height in 1977 (at 8.4% of the active population) and dropped regularly thereafter to less than 5% by mid-1980. It rose again in 1982 and 1983. Compared with men, female workers are particularly vulnerable to unemployment, as are migrants and those workers entering the labour market for the first time (Muñoz et al. 1977, Pommier 1982: 354). Certain districts like Netzahualcóyotl have particularly high levels of unemployment and underemployment. Although there has been an important rise in un- employment and work was not easily come by during 1977–8 and 1982–3, the situation is almost certainly better in the capital than elsewhere.[6] Also the rate of female participation in the economy of the Federal District is almost twice the national average (García et al. 1982: 35). In part this has come about by the expansion of maquiladora-type industries established in Mexico City over the past decade.

Nevertheless, wages are not high. Despite the fact that the majority enjoy regular employment most are poorly paid. According to one sample, 41% of those employed earned the official minimum wage or less, while 66% of the total economically active population earned less than twice the official mini- mum wage (Muñoz et al. 1977: 87–9). The minimum wage offers a subsistence income and in June 1984 stood at just under five dollars a day.

In terms of social welfare the city does better than the provinces. The Federal District has three times as many doctors per capita than elsewhere. The population covered by some form of social security is twice as high as the national average. School facilities are better in the Federal District and children are not only more likely to attend school, but also to complete the various stages of schooling. Similarly the lion's share of investment resources for public housing have been directed towards the Metropolitan Area. Between 1963 and 1975, for example, 58% of the public housing units constructed for the poor and for lower-middle income groups were built within the Metropolitan Area (Garza & Schteingart 1978).

Problems for Mexico City's population
Although relatively privileged compared with the rest of the population, life in Mexico City also entails many difficulties. Pollution is a constant problem. Located in an upland basin, the city suffers from frequent temperature inversions which prevent the dispersal of pollutants. As a result, smog has reduced daily visibility from an average 15 kilometres in 1967 to between 4 and 6 kilometres today. The dried-up lake bed of Texcoco creates dust storms during the dry season, while in central areas the population is also subject to the fumes emanating from congested city streets. Fox (1972) describes the distribution of

mortality and morbidity rates for large districts of the city, and notes that death
in children from bronchial disorders in the east of the city was twice the overall
average.

Transport is another major problem. Buses carry 44% of daily passenger
traffic in the Federal District and although diesel fuel is subsidized and fares are
low, the buses themselves are slow, overcrowded and uncomfortable. The
Metro is modern, fast and cheap, but despite recent additions to its network it
remains limited in its coverage. On balance it seems that public transport costs
people more in the way of time than money. In 1979 a major new rapid-transit
road system was opened within the Federal District (*ejes viales*), which has
speeded the flow of traffic considerably. However, in large part the beneficiaries
of this programme have been private car owners.

Access to housing and service provision are major problems which will be
examined in detail in the following chapters. Suffice to record here that a large
part of the built-up area has developed illegally, and comprises irregular
settlements, most of which are only partially serviced. Since 1952 the self-built
low-income settlements (*colonias populares*) increased from 23% of the built-up
area and 14% of the population to more than half the total population and built-
up area (Ward 1981b: 39). Generally dwellings in the older settlements are more
consolidated and have a greater range of services such as water, electricity,
drainage and paving. Socially too they are more mixed and many householders
are non-owners. In the inner-city areas most poor people rent accommodation,
often in cramped one- or two-roomed tenements with shared services (*vecindades*).
As we shall observe later in this book, although opportunities for land acquisition are becoming fewer, the coverage of services is better in the city than it is
in the provinces. However, this is more a reflection on the poor allocation of
resources elsewhere than a commendation for housing conditions in Mexico
City.

City administration and financial resources
The Federal District bureaucracy has grown and become more complex in
recent years. In addition the budget exercised by the DDF almost quadrupled in
real terms between 1972 and 1982. From the early 1970s, Echeverría sought to
initiate some decentralization of functions from City Hall to the *delegaciones*, and
this process has been accelerated by subsequent administrations. Although
some important functions remain centralized and the Federal District mayor
continues to determine annual appropriations made to the *delegaciónes*, it is clear
from the growth in their budgets that they enjoy greater financial responsibility
and influence than in the past. The share of the overall *delegacíon* budget that each
receives appears to be related to population resident in the area and changes little
from year to year.

Traditionally the high-spending departments have been water, drainage
and public works. During Echeverría's administration heavy investment was
undertaken in the deep drainage scheme and in extensions to the primary water

supply network. Once completed, investment declined somewhat and some of the cash was handed over to *delegaciones*, which became partly responsible for developing domestic supplies. Public works consumed a particularly large slice of the budget in 1979 as Mayor Hank González concentrated resources upon his *ejes viales* road-building programme. After this ended large sums continued to be spent on extensions to the Metro system, and COVITUR (the transport commission which was responsible for these works) consumed between one-quarter and one-third of the total Federal District expenditure between 1980 and 1983.

Largely as a result of these major investment projects indebtedness rose steeply during 1980–2. Significantly the 1979 annual statement of accounts is accompanied for the first time by a statement explaining the dramatic rise in certain items of expenditure (notably public works). This is justified in terms of the investment that was required to fulfil the requirements of the National Urban Development Plan passed in 1978. As we shall observe in the following chapter this is not the only occasion upon which urban planning has been used retrospectively to justify political decisions.

The 1982 crisis quickly cut into the programme approved by City Hall. Devaluation of the peso in February meant that all departments had to plan for immediate cuts. These were compounded in a further round of budget reductions initiated in August. Not for the first time local mayors appealed to residents to help reduce the burden of costs of local public works by contributing their labour through self-help and mutual aid.

A primary task of Mayor Ramón Aguirre (an accountant by training), who was appointed in 1982, was to straighten out the city's accounts. Immediately he took office he pledged that there would be no more lavish and expensive building programmes and that only the most urgently required sections of the then unfinished Metro would be completed in the short term. His first two years in office had limited impact. Some administrative reorganization aimed at diluting the power base of the large-spending departments took place, as did further decentralization of the *delegaciones*, as witnessed by their additional budgets. However, it is debatable whether this had led to a streamlining of functions: in many respects overlaps appear to have increased. Public spending on urban projects has been extremely small and criticism mounted in 1984, during heavy flooding brought about by inadequate operation and cleaning of the city's drainage system. It remains to be seen whether or not Mayor Ramón Aguirre will keep his word or whether he will be obliged to embark on a public spending programme as part of a general reflationary package from 1985–6 onwards. Obviously the September 1985 earthquake will demand some shift of investment into a rebuilding programme.

Taken overall, therefore, Mexico presents an excellent opportunity for the analysis of the nature of social welfare provision. Its population is large, growing rapidly and for the most part poor. It is also predominantly urban and therefore reasonably concentrated in population centres that are integrated within the wider economic and political structure. More significantly Mexico's recent economic development displays many of the attributes of a rapidly developing country. Highly dependent, it has passed through a phase of heavy investment in import-substituting activities. It has also endeavoured to extend 'backward linkages' by developing some heavy industry based around steel and chemicals. Today though, industrial development is increasingly capital intensive and 'high-tech', aggravating further the difficulties of accommodating labour within the manufacturing sector. Nevertheless, the extensive nature of Mexico's manufacturing sector means that there is a large blue-collar 'proletariat', a small proportion of which is highly skilled and relatively highly paid. The extent to which these social groups have negotiated social welfare advantages will provide valuable insight into the relationship between social and economic development.

Given Mexico's erratic and uneven growth in recent years the ability of different governments to develop 'social welfare' has often conflicted with other development priorities. It will be salutary to analyse the factors which led to greater or lesser commitment to the social sector by past administrations. Nor has Mexico's overall economic growth led to dramatic improvement for its working classes. Social welfare provision is as much an issue still as it was 20 years ago. Indeed it might be argued that the need is greater than ever given the economic crisis, declining opportunities for secure and well-paid employment, deteriorating real wages and rising costs of basic subsistence goods. In the following chapter I try to identify which groups are most influential in shaping policy and to show how the decision-making process has shifted in recent years towards a more 'technocratic' style of management.

Notes

1 For example, whereas cropland under *ejidos* accounted for only 13% in 1930, by 1940 this proportion had increased to 47%.
2 Needler (1982: 110) notes in extenuation that part of the increased development of indebtedness was due to the importation of equipment for the oil industry itself, and partly due to goods such as transportation and road construction made necessary by the rapid economic growth attendant on the oil boom. It may be seen, therefore, as a short-term problem.
3 I am grateful to Laurence Whitehead (personal communication) for providing an assessment about the published 1985 government budget allocations. It appeared, then, that his earlier (1984) proposition about the inevitability of reflation is beginning to be sustained.
4 It has been suggested that President Echeverría's inner Cabinet deliberately withheld information about the huge size of oil reserves as they preferred to employ a 'rhetorical "nationalist" tack of verbally assaulting the TNCs' [Trans National Corporations] "looting" of Mexico' (Cockcroft 1983: 261).
5 Iglesias (1984: 192) in *Comericio Exterior*, calculated using data provided by the Secretaría de Trabajo.
6 Chant (1984: 80) notes that in Querétaro some 25% of the industrial workforce lost their jobs during the latter part of the 1982 crisis.

3 Politics, government and planning

If the economy has undergone profound change during the 1970s and 1980s, so too has the nature of the Mexican political system. Broadly, the political and governmental structures have drawn apart during the period so that the careers and personnel engaged in each overlap less and less. In particular the government is manned increasingly by technocrats rather than by 'old style' politicians. In this chapter my aim is to analyse the nature of decision making in Mexico, and to use the case of urban planning in an attempt to understand contemporary bureaucratic and political performance.

Political and governmental structures in Mexico: who governs?

Since the 1930s Mexico has been dominated by a single party, which has evolved through several stages from its early origins as the National Revolutionary Party (PNR), to become the Mexican Revolutionary Party (PRM) under President Cárdenas, and finally in 1945 to emerge in its definitive form as the Institutionalized Revolutionary Party (PRI). During the metamorphosis the party shed much of the influence of the military that had been important in the post-revolutionary decade and took on board a greater representation of labour, subsequently broadened to include middle-income and 'popular' groups. It has been described as 'a party of consensus, moderation and stability' (Needler 1982: 29). The significance is that since its formation it has always been the governing party. The president is a PRI 'candidate' and wins an overwhelming proportion of the vote. Similarly PRI senators and deputies dominate almost all elections for the legislature. The PRI colours and the national flag are identical. Little wonder, therefore, that the popular impression is that the PRI is, in effect, the government. While this impression is deliberately fostered by the PRI it is a false one. I believe that it is important for the purpose of analysis to draw a careful distinction between the party political apparatus and the government bureaucracy (and in particular the Executive wing of government). Although there is some occasional overlap, they are usually quite distinct in terms of personnel, career tracks, functions, and access to resources. In the following sections I examine the importance of political parties in general, and the PRI in particular, in exercising influence over decision making and the allocation of resources for social welfare provision. A key question is whether political parties in Mexico provide effective channels for influencing decision making.

Party politics in Mexico: the growth of genuine opposition?

The Mexican political system is generally considered to be authoritarian. It displays a low level of political mobilization and limited pluralism in which the contest for power is restricted to supporters of the regime. The latter possesses a 'mentality' rather than a clear ideology (Smith 1979: 53; see also Needler, 1982). Inevitably, in a system such as this, considerable importance is placed upon election results as a source of legitimacy for the governing elite.

Throughout its history the official party (the PRI) has received overwhelming electoral support – almost always more than 75% of the turnout at presidential elections (Smith 1979: 55, Cockcroft 1983: 307). Despite this fact a dilemma faced by the PRI is how to retain absolute control and sustain existing levels of support while at the same time stimulating sufficient interest among the opposition in competitive electoral politics. This has been resolved on the one hand by ensuring support from the grassroots through its tripartite party structure (see below) and by rigging the ballot-box. On the other hand, while competitive party politics has been narrowly circumscribed the presence and activity of opposition parties has been carefully sustained and sometimes sponsored by the PRI. Indeed, the greatest threat to the PRI's cultivation of a democratic facade is posed by abstentions (González Casanova 1970). In order to encourage people to vote there is intense propaganda for elections which are held on a Sunday, and the sale of liquor is banned on polling day. There is also a widespread popular fear that failure to vote might lead to some sort of penalty. (Refusal by the authorities to grant a passport application is one widely feared sanction, although I know of no cases where it has been applied.)

If the PRI are considered to occupy the middle-left ground of the political spectrum in Mexico then the only concerted opposition, at least until recently, has been provided by the right-wing National Action Party (PAN). Established to combat the left-wing tendencies adopted by Cárdenas, the PAN attracts support from conservative business circles, provincial and large city middle classes, and from the Catholic Church (Cockcroft 1983: 305). Although it has never won more than 15% of the vote, it regularly wins a few electoral districts by majority vote. These may comprise large cities such as Ciudad Juárez. Its strongholds are located primarily in the north of the country and in Mérida in the Yucatán.

But for the most part in the past the opposition in Mexico has been stage-managed by the PRI (González Casanova 1970) to such an extent that by the late 1960s the need to revitalize the political structure and to restore the legitimacy of the governing elite was widely felt.[1] Political reforms were initiated in 1973 and extended further in 1977. Two important changes were introduced. First, the reforms provided for the registration of a host of new parties, most of which were left-wing. The most important among these were the Mexican Communist Party (PCM), the Socialist Workers' Party (PST) and the Mexican Workers' Party (PMT). On the right, and far more populist than the PAN, is the Mexican Democratic Party (PDM). Secondly, the size of Congress was increased, and one-quarter of the 400 seats were given to opposition parties to be allocated on the basis of proportional representation of the votes received.

These initiatives had an important effect upon the political process. In 1982, 50 of the opposition seats went to the PAN, while the remainder were shared between the PDM (12), PST (11), PPS (10) and the PSUM (a PCM-led coalition of several left-wing parties; 17). While the PRI's pre-eminence is assured and a clear majority in the Congress is guaranteed, there is now greater incentive for opposition parties to participate in elections. Their representation in the Chamber of Deputies has sharpened the level of debate and criticism of government policy. Although a carefully controlled minority, they provide an important channel for registering political dissent. Whether or not this ultimately makes any appreciable difference to the position of working-class Mexicans is open to question. However, the *apertura democrática* initiated by President Echeverría and extended by López Portillo represents a significant step in opening political franchise and expression in Mexico. But we should recognize that its purpose was not to reduce the authority and role of the PRI but rather to enhance and sustain it.

The PRI

Given the prominence of the official party it is necessary to examine the extent to which it wields influence over policy making. The party is built around three sectors: the National Confederation of Farmworkers (CNC); a labour sector (CTM), and a socially heterogeneous Confederation of 'Popular' Organizations (CNOP) comprising middle-class professions such as teachers as well as local organizations representing low-income settlements, tradesmen's unions and so on. Each of these sectors represents a solid grassroots organized on a strictly hierarchical basis, with minimal horizontal linkage either between sectors or individual federations. Thus all party or federation bosses look upwards for their orders and often compete openly against those on a similar level to themselves (Schers 1972, Eckstein 1977). Although they are all within the same umbrella organization (the PRI), this hierarchical structure offers enormous scope for political manipulation from above. Up-and-coming party militants can be set against one another; those who show particular promise may be promoted and lifted into a bigger pond; those who become too powerful can be frozen out and isolated (Schers 1972, Smith 1979).

The incorporation of this mass base of grassroots support into the governing party might lead one to believe that the structure provides the means whereby working-class interests are represented upwards, through the executive com-mittee of each sector, to the PRI executive, and thence to shape government policy directly. However, this 'aggregate interest model' (Scott 1964, Hun-tingdon 1968) does not seem to apply. In fact, the party has minimal power over decision making and only limited access to resources (Padgett 1966, Hansen 1974, Eckstein 1977, Smith 1979). The PRI's role is principally to provide a career structure for up-and-coming politicians; to conciliate the negotiation of jobs (i.e. patronage) given the high turnover of electoral posts every three and six years; and, finally, to ensure the legitimacy of the government by mobilizing support at the polls. Indeed, I believe that one can go further to argue that the PRI's function to the state is to provide political and social control (Hansen 1974, Eckstein 1977). This is achieved by concentrating power in the hands of a few sector bosses at the top, by controlling the selection of personnel, by the co-option of leaders and organizations, and by the manipulation of factions within the PRI.

For electoral purposes the PRI is organized at four levels into sectional, municipal, state and national committees. Deputies elected to the legislature have little or no local responsibility to their constituents. The national president, state governors and municipal presidents are 'unveiled' and only then does the PRI step in to run their election campaigns. As we shall observe below, selection to 'run' for these executive posts is not a preserve of the PRI. Although some municipal presidents and even governors may have held previous elective offices or positions within the party apparatus, they are equally likely to come from a career track outside it. Generally speaking the higher the post the less likely it is that the individual has been directly dependent in the past upon PRI patronage for a job. None of the three presidents considered in detail in this book had run for electoral office prior to being chosen as candidate.

Nor does the fact that these elected government officials depend upon the PRI for stage-managing their electoral campaigns usually shape their subsequent behaviour in allocating resources preferentially to PRI constituents. This is for two reasons. First, the individual is aware that he or she must serve primarily as a government functionary and that any party allegiance should be placed after other considerations. Primarily he or she will be judged on ability to pacify all interest groups and to minimize public dissension or upwellings of unrest. If favours are solicited by a party official they will be met only in so far as the personal weight and influence of the PRI member making the request demands it, and the extent to which the individual executive officer feels that his or her future career may be firmly located within the party political apparatus. Secondly, resources at the disposal of state governors and especially municipal presidents are very limited. Funds remain firmly in the hands of the federal government and its agencies. It is to them that elected officials look and not to the PRI, which has no ready access to or influence over federal expenditure. The irony is that as part of its normal endeavours to co-opt and integrate local groups, the PRI deliberately encourages the impression that it has this special access and influence. In fact, close association and integration under the party's umbrella is likely to reduce the probability of a group getting what it wants simply because, once co-opted, they become subject to PRI orthodoxy, which seeks to reduce the level of demand making upon the system (Cornelius 1975, Eckstein 1977).

In future, as electoral districts become more hotly contested by the new political parties, and as the state continues to demand that the PRI deliver the vote on behalf of the government and executive officers, it seems likely that the pressure for preferential treatment of groups affiliated to the official party will grow. There is a basic and growing contradiction, therefore, between the state's desire for *apertura política* which requires that the PRI not be seen to have privileged access to resources, and the ability of the party to guarantee future support without being granted greater opportunities for exercising patronage.

The government and the Executive

If the official party has relatively little influence over national policy, we may ask how policy is determined. To evaluate this question we must look briefly, first, at the structure of government and, secondly, at the way in which different groups articulate their interests and the factors that determine their success.

The Mexican government comprises a federal system with state governors and state legislatures. The president holds office for a non-renewable six-year term and appoints Cabinet members and ambassadors subject to ratification by the Senate.[2] Although this structure broadly corresponds to that of the USA, the reality is rather different (Needler 1982: 86). Congress is very docile, even if less so than in the past, and passes all government legislation. The power of the president is enormous and his person and office are not usually openly criticized (an exception being the hostile criticism from northern business interest circles to Echeverría's policies; Saldivar 1981).

Appointments to Cabinet and other offices are made according to a wide range of criteria. People are selected for their personal loyalty and past support. The president must also aim to reconcile a wide range of interest groups and seek to ensure that all are included in his Cabinet (Needler 1982: 90). However, to balance this and to keep a cross check on the actions of ministers he will often appoint his own people to sub-ministerial posts. Until restrictions were imposed in 1983, nepotism and sinecures for relations and friends were widespread. Increasingly, though, appointees must be professionally competent. Important jobs require sensitive handling and banana skins must be carefully avoided. In Díaz Serrano's administrative mishandling of PEMEX he badly betrayed President López Portillo's trust in appointing his close friend to run the agency.

Differences in ideology are not usually the basis for determining the constitution of different 'groups' in Mexican politics. Rather, groups are organized into 'leader–follower' alliances sometimes called *camarillas* (Grindle 1977). These may be best envisaged as teams which form around a particular person and which move as that individual moves between different posts in government. This explains why the same people may appear in such unlikely consecutive positions as CONASUPO, the Ministry of Health and Welfare, and the State of Mexico government (Grindle 1977: 57). Each *camarilla* actually comprises a series of layers with 'leaders' and sub-teams at each level. Ultimately, however, they lead to the same top politician. Occasionally *camarillas* overlap, leading upwards to two influential leaders. In such a case a close alliance would usually exist between the two, and the sharing out of jobs and placement of personnel would be done by agreement. In these cases working for one boss after previously working for the other is acceptable. Otherwise transfer across groups is not tolerated and among the 'rules' of behaviour the greatest breach is disloyalty (Grindle 1977, Smith 1979).

Although these groups are not ideologically based they may be tied to particular interest groups (Cockcroft 1983: 212). Strangely, given their importance, little is known about the constitution of such groups. For non-Mexicans the complex web of *camarillas* is one of the most difficult and inaccessible concepts. Indeed, my experience is that for Mexicans, too, an understanding is often implicit and acquired gradually over many years rather than explicit and learned. In essence, political 'nous' in Mexico is the ability to recognize and predict the implications of any single action for competing *camarillas*.

Over the past two decades an important shift has taken place in the type of person who gains top public office. Gone are the old-style politicians from provincial and often military backgrounds (Needler 1982). While the ruling elite continue to be drawn from among the wealthy, well-known families, they are increasingly likely to be from the central regions of the country and from the Federal District in particular. Increasingly, too, they are 'technocrats', though clearly if they are to advance significantly they must also show political acumen.[3] Most will have gone through the National University (UNAM); some will have taught there. While law used to be the most popular form of professional training, this has widened to encompass engineering, architecture and economics, usually supplemented by postgraduate experience abroad (Needler 1982: 81). Presidents Echeverría and López Portillo were born in the Federal District and became close friends as contemporaries at the UNAM Law School. Although a native of the State of Colima, De la Madrid grew up in Mexico City, went to the UNAM where he read economics, and later to Harvard. A similar pattern emerges for recent ministerial appointments. Inevitably, the people whom recent presidents have sought to bring into their administrations reflect similar backgrounds and expertise.

Just as there is relatively little movement between the party political and the governmental bureaucracies so, too, is there little career overlap with the private sector. As Needler (1982: 83) writes:

> The economic elite which dominates the private sector is based not primarily in Mexico City, but in Monterrey. Its family names are different from those of the governing class. Its children attend not the National University but the *polytecnicos* [sic] and the schools of management. There is no practice of recruiting top people from the private sector to serve in cabinet-level positions, as in the United States.

Compared with the USA the Mexican bureaucracy is vast and has expanded considerably since 1970. In 1975 it comprised 18 ministries, 123 decentralized agencies, 292 public enterprises, 187 official commissions and 160 development trusts (Grindle 1977: 3). Since that date attempts have been made to reduce the overall number and to co-ordinate more closely their activities by making them responsible to 'heads of sectors'. But in several ways a distended bureaucracy may be highly functional to the state. By providing jobs it facilitates the circulation of patronage. It creates opportunities for manipulation by the Executive: personnel posing a threat can be 'frozen out' or their authority undermined by the creation of a duplicate agency; support can be bestowed upon certain agencies and subtly withdrawn from others. Also, an intricate bureaucracy with ample red tape slows down the outflow of resources while at the same time creating an appearance of being 'busy' and overworked.

Another feature of government is the way in which the six-year cycle creates an important dynamic of its own. Broadly the first two years comprise the co-ordination of teams, establishing new policies and disassociating oneself from those of one's predecessor, and securing adequate finance to carry through one's programmes (Grindle 1977). These are carried out during years three, four and five after which people begin to look around and get close to those who are likely to figure prominently in the forthcoming administration. Once one of the existing Cabinet has been named as the new candidate (in effect president-elect), then all bets are off. Those overly associated with the 'losers' are said to be 'burned' (*quemado*), and know that they will not figure significantly in the next government.[4] Although it would be incorrect to suggest that during the last year the president is a lame duck, within government agencies and ministries few new actions are undertaken and most work concentrates on completing projects already underway.

Bureaucracy performance: political and technical rationalities
I have already referred to a growing technocratic composition of those holding high public office in Mexico. But does this mean also that the agencies and ministries that they man are run in a more technocratic manner? While I would accept that the adoption of a technocratic style clearly represents a 'political' position with political implications, one can, I believe, make a useful distinction between bureaucracies which function according to 'rational-technical' criteria and those whose primary object is 'partisan-political' in nature.[5] Obviously in some cases the overt functions and style will be technical, although the covert *raison d'être* is political. We will meet examples of both types of agency or government department throughout this book so it is important that we distinguish carefully between them.

'Functional rationality comprises an exclusive use of technical criteria in making decisions and the key consideration is one of efficiency' (Friedmann 1965). In contrast politicians are guided by political rationality which implies that decisions are formulated upon a basis of 'who benefits and who pays the cost of a particular decision' (Rivera Ortiz 1976: 150). To elaborate: 'In a political decision . . . action never is based on the merits of a proposal but always on who makes it and who opposes it. . . . A course of action which corrects economic or social deficiencies, but increases political difficulties must be rejected, while an action which contributes to political improvement is desirable even if it is not entirely sound from an economic and social standpoint' (Diesing 1962). In Mexico 'political' actions are not simply those relating to political parties. As we have already observed Mexican politics revolves around groups and Diesing's statement must be conceived in those terms.

In reality these are 'ideal-type' extremes and agencies will fall somewhere on a continuum between the two poles. Broadly, for the purposes of my analysis in this book a technical bureaucracy is one which is autonomous, stable, accountable and objective (Gilbert & Ward 1985). It is autonomous in the sense that once overall policy is established by the president the agency is free to make day-to-day decisions without interference from extra-agency actors, and its budget is either self-financing or protected from constant modification. Stability implies that policy is modified only at regular intervals – at the beginning of each *sexenio*, for example – and budgets change no more than once a year. Accountability means that the agency is expected to perform specific measurable tasks 'respectably'. Failure will result in a loss of autonomy, withdrawal of resources or the creation of a rival agency to perform similar functions. Objectivity requires that the agency will discharge its business primarily according to set rules and routines without taking account of the specific individuals affected by any decision. Queues are established according to strict rules which make queue jumping difficult. A politicized agency presents characteristics converse to those outlined above: it will lack autonomy, be unstable, be constantly accountable and it will not be objective.

Policy making: who rules?
We have observed that public policy in Mexico does not emerge from within the ranks of the official party, nor from the legislature. Neither is it the product of a clear ideological stance. Mexico watchers tend to have their own particular analogy that best describes the nature of the political process. Some see it as a card game in which different interests participate – occasionally winning a little, sometimes losing, but never destroying everything by kicking over the table (Needler 1982: 71). Others see it as 'marriage', governed and delimited by certain rules yet actually worked out on a day-to-day basis of negotiation (Purcell & Purcell 1980). In fact it is very difficult to say precisely how policy is formulated as discussions take place behind closed doors 'beyond the purview of the general public and the rank-and-file adherents of the official party' (Grindle 1977: 7).

The political system may be envisaged as a delicate balancing act involving all elite interests incorporated into a 'political bargain' which is constantly renewed in day-to-day action (Purcell & Purcell 1980: 194–5). It is 'inclusionary' in so far as all groups or interests are represented, though inevitably any sharp change in policy will advance certain interests at the expense of others. The adverse effects of such action are usually minimized, and a tacitly agreed aim is to avoid the existence of outright 'winners' and 'losers'. However, every administration creates certain imbalances and the expectancy is that these will be redressed in the following administration. This helps to explain the tendency to shift back and forth between 'activist' and 'consolidatory' presidents (*ibid.* 1980: 222). The critical task of the president is to strike and maintain that balance within his administration (Smith 1979: 303–4).

Key groups incorporated into the governing elite are, of course, the leaderships of the CTM, CNC and CNOP, but they are likely to be accorded significance without predominance. The coalition can ill afford to alienate the *campesino* sector or organized labour, but the degree to which the Executive is prepared actively to support the interests of these groups depends upon the balance of forces within the coalition at any time (Purcell & Purcell 1980: 202). Also closely involved is the private sector. Opinions differ about the degree to which they actually form part of the governing bloc and most analysts see a clear separation between government and business interests (Smith 1979: 214, Needler 1982, but cf. Cockcroft 1983: 210). However, there are several state/corporatist entities such as the Confederation of Chambers of Industry (CONCAMIN) and of Commerce (CONCANACO) which are designed to inform government decisions directly. Equally there are numerous other independent 'voices', such as the Employers' Confederation (COPARMEX) and that of manufacturing industries (CANACINTRA). Undoubtedly soundings are taken from these groups but policy is essentially decided within the Executive – the president, his private office, and bureaucrats whom he sees fit to involve. While decisions may be taken that hurt certain interests, the 'bargain' demands acquiesence on the understanding that imbalances will eventually be redressed. If any group breaks this agreement then they are likely to be 'disciplined' in one of several ways open to the government (Purcell & Purcell 1980).

To a large extent this arrangement has served the Mexican state well. Particularly when the economy is expanding it is fairly easy for the state to make the necessary pay-offs to appease different social groups. But as we have already observed the past three administrations have not enjoyed a smooth economic passage, and I want briefly to describe the policy directions adopted by each. I am conscious that so far this account has identified the various elements of the Mexican governmental and political systems but that I have not generated a 'feel' for the nature of each administration. This is an important backcloth to an understanding of the detailed policy analysis undertaken throughout the remainder of the book.

The character of policy directions over three sexenios

Upon taking office Echeverría's primary concern was to shift the direction of the economy away from the 'stabilizing development' model towards one of 'shared development'. To do this he promoted greater state involvement and intervention in economic development, introduced tax reforms, and created a host of welfare and development agencies that would assist in redistributing some of the benefits of growth. Secondly, he recognized the need to revitalize the political process that had become stale and ossified. Thus he set in motion the *apertura política* which opened up opportunities for greater participation of opposition parties within the Mexican political system.

There were several reasons for this approach. In part it reflected Echeverría's strong and forceful personality, and his style of working which was intensive, highly pressurized and frenetic. More importantly, there were sound economic reasons for change as the traditional model of development was proving incapable of generating a wider distribution of the benefits of growth. In the words of one of his close collaborators of the time, Mexico was eating the goose that laid the golden egg (Tello 1978). We must also remember that Echeverría was Minister of the Interior under the previous government. More than anyone else he had his finger on the pulse of social unrest during the late 1960s. The Doctors' protest movement of 1968, the Tlatelolco demonstrations and massacre, rural unrest and guerrilla organizations, mobilizations by the urban poor for basic services and housing, and the huge social welfare problems identified in the 1970 census convinced him of the need to act.

Inevitably, however, neither his policies nor his brand of revolutionary rhetoric and demagogy endeared him to the business sector, who resisted many of the measures he adopted. Partly as a result of this opposition many of the more far-reaching proposals contained in legislation were subsequently diluted or dropped altogether (Hansen 1974, Saldivar 1981). In an attempt to overcome resistance from right-wing business interests Echeverría used patron–client links to mobilize the poor to attend rallies in support of his public pronouncements. This heightened the conflict still further, and the last months of his administration were marked by tit-for-tat political strife as each side attempted to out-manoeuvre the other. Big business withdrew its capital to foreign accounts, reduced industrial production and issued strong anti-government press releases through the Chambers of Commerce and Industry. For his part Echeverría adopted a belligerent attitude, denounced this business-based opposition as anti-nationalist oligarchs and gave his blessing to land invasions of large farms in Sonora. The night before his final State of the Nation address he was forced to devalue the peso and there was financial chaos until he left office. Even his relinquishing the presidency was in doubt: rumours of a military coup were rife, or that Echeverría would suspend the transfer of power to the president-elect. When he gave up office on 1 December there was an almost audible sigh of relief (Smith 1979).

López Portillo responded cautiously. His primary concern was to shift the political balance back into the middle ground as a means of restoring confidence, and to capitalize upon the exploitation of oil resources for national development. In the short term his simple accession did much to restore confidence. He also contracted financial support from the IMF and with it was obliged to adopt an austerity programme. Unemployment was high, and real wages dropped, as did public sector expenditure. López Portillo's style was more intellectual – almost professorial – and benign. He sought to streamline the bureaucracy through a major administrative reform, thereby making it more efficient. He also recognized that the earlier political reform had not gone far enough and took steps to open things up even further.

By 1978 confidence had been restored, the enormous extent of oil reserves was becoming public knowledge and international finance was almost falling over itself in wishing to make loans to Mexico. López Portillo quietly threw off the shackles of IMF stringency measures and reflated. Government expenditure increased, the production of oil rose dramatically, the economy began to grow and jobs were created. These were heady days in which a false optimism reigned and, as we observed earlier, the economy overheated and foundered in 1982 when the price of oil dropped overnight and inflation forced major devaluations of the currency. López Portillo gave the appearance of an intensely disappointed and rather haunted man. In a last ditch, desperate measure he nationalized the private banking system, a move seen by some as a significant attempt to tighten state control over exchange; others view it as primarily a diversionary tactic that would brighten the president's by then very tarnished public image.

As with the previous two presidents, incoming De la Madrid was an intimate friend of his predecessor, yet as usual, he was obliged to distance himself both socially and politically from the outgoing president. In this case we do not have the whole of his *sexenio* upon which to reflect, but only the four years comprising his electoral campaign and first three years in office. Nevertheless a clear impression emerges.

In late 1982 Mexico faced its worst financial and economic crisis ever. Moreover, this time there were no reserve funds that could be dipped into, nor the possibility of receiving credit using oil reserves as collateral. Quite the opposite: the repayments on the debt were due and creditors were extremely concerned to know whether or not they would be repaid. Once again the new Executive rose to meet the challenge and one cannot help being impressed by the way in which the political process 'throws up' a man suited to the time. To a certain extent, of course, De la Madrid shaped his image according to the task that he confronted, and when he was actually selected as official candidate late in 1981 few could have foreseen precisely what was in store. Yet his technocratic, well-educated, upright, moral and clean-living image combined with an almost fanatical determination to get the economy in order was precisely what the private sector and the international community wanted from a Mexican president in 1983.

As soon as he entered the presidency De la Madrid introduced a National Development Plan comprising an immediate emergency programme of crisis management and a longer-term strategy to induce structural changes within the economy (Mexico SPP 1983). As regards the former, Treasury Minister Silva Herzog was instructed to negotiate an immediate extension on those debts for which repayment was due. This required IMF involvement and an austerity package was adopted comprising, as we have seen, severe wage restraint, cuts in public expenditure, rising unemployment, and further devaluations. The principal objective of these measures was to reduce inflation from its annual 100% level. The president also sought to tie up many of the loose ends relating to the expropriation of the banks and announced that ex-bankers would be allowed to re-acquire minority holdings in the various banks, but that the latter would remain under government control. In an attempt to combat the social unrest created by the austerity measures a range of actions were undertaken. These included preferential treatment to agencies providing social welfare and housing. A Planning Law was also passed which set in motion a National Democratic Planning System, part of which led to a nationwide consultation aimed at integrating popular opinion and public involvement in policy making (the *consulta popular*). A morality campaign (*renovación moral*) was instigated to counter corruption, reduce nepotism and to raise efficiency within the public sector. Many leading figures from the previous administration were indicted and imprisoned on corruption charges; others who had fled the country were sought using extradition orders.

The longer-term strategy involved further debt restructuring, which was achieved finally in August 1984; the stimulation of economic growth; investment in productive enterprises, especially those that generate employment, reform of the fiscal system and the stabilization of exchange rates, and so on.

From the outside, Mexico is generally considered to be a success story. Internally the picture during 1983 was one of labour disputes and conflict that was met by stony-faced intransigence on the part of government. Many strikes collapsed, real wages remained depressed, unemployment was rising. Recently however, inflation has begun to decline and there are forecasts of between 3% and 4% growth in GDP in 1985. The impression is given of a reorganization of the bureaucracy but it is often paper shuffling: the redistribution of functions often associated with decentralization programmes. However, until departments begin spending it will be difficult to judge whether greater efficiency has actually been achieved. Certainly much of the blatant abuse associated with posts in officialdom has been reduced. Although the president painted a rather too rosy picture of the nation's health in his second State of the Nation address (1 September 1984), it seems that Mexico is turning the corner. Whether the remaining four years will consist of more of the same or see a genuine improvement and some measure of reflation is an open question. Personally I believe that we will see a little of both, but that the benefits accruing to the majority of the population will be barely discernible.

The politics of planning in Mexico

The emergence of urban planning during the 1970s exemplifies *par excellence* both the technocratization of the decision-making process and the way in which the bureaucracy functions to fulfil political needs. The latter may include opportunities for the Executive to extend its patronage through public appointments, as well as ample room in which to manipulate competing factions within the bureaucracy. Plans and planning may also justify decisions that have already been taken behind closed doors. Last, but not least, it creates an overall ideology of urban management that is conducive to ensure the passivity and the compliance of the poor.

In Mexico, as elsewhere in Latin America, urban planning is a relatively recent phenomenon.[6] Although national planning structures existed during the 1950s in a few countries such as Colombia (1953), Nicaragua (1952) and Ecuador (1954), and planning teams existed to administer regional and special projects, planning throughout this period was structurally weak. In part planners were to blame for they saw themselves, somehow, as 'above' the institutional political system (Cibotti et al 1974: 40). They were overly concerned with technical criteria and regulations and often ignored the reality of the ways in which decision making occurs throughout Latin America. They failed, therefore, to identify the role of dominant groups in determining development processes (Kaplan 1972: 28).

Planning also posed a threat to the traditional forms of political mediation exercised through patronage. As Wynia states (1972: 84), 'planning is an orderly process, traditional mediation of political conflict is not'. For politicians the priority is political control, not the efficiency of development (Gilbert 1981b). Politicians need to be able to exercise discretionary control over the allocation of resources and to be able to act in a personalistic way. In Mexico the precarious 'balancing act' to which I referred earlier suggests little sympathy from politicians for a decision-making framework influenced by planners. A further constraint was the fear by many politicians that they would become over-dependent upon *técnicos*. Traditionally in Latin America the latter did not form part of the president's personal trusted team, and an Executive is unlikely to view favourably a growing dependence upon a body of technicians whose data processing and information handling is indispensable. Put simply, the presidential calculus may be firmly invested against formal incorporation of the planning process (Wynia 1972: 193).

Finally, there was a widespread fear that the existence of plans would, inevitably, lead to a greater dissemination of information to the public. In societies where decisions are often made behind closed doors according to highly particularistic criteria, the last thing that decision makers want is informed criticism. Theoretically, too, planning requires active participation of the population at large. It should be open, democratic and participative. It would be naive to suggest that these epithets apply fully to planning processes in the UK or in the United States, but it is certainly anathema in most Latin American countries today.

Despite these barriers the importance of urban planning in Mexico has grown since 1970. As part of his strategy of 'shared development' Echeverría developed a wide range of planning activities through the creation of rural development agencies like PIDER, and through schemes to promote the decentralization of industry and the stimulation of development 'poles' outside Mexico City. From 1973 onwards the Executive gave increasing weight to urban-industrial policies culminating in a Human Settlements Law passed in 1976. This created the basis for the state to intervene in a consistent and integrated way in the planning of human settlements, and it identified the levels of responsibility for policy making – federal, state, conurbation and municipality.

López Portillo consolidated planning activity within a Ministry of Human Settlements and Public Works (SAHOP). Within a year a National Urban Development Plan was published which aimed to confront the huge disparities in the distribution of national population. The plan created a national framework of 11 integrated urban zones with programmes designed to shape efficient urban systems within each. Population centres were subject to policies of a stimulus; consolidation; or ordering and regulation. Mexico City, needless to say, fell within the final category. The function of the Human Settlements Ministry was to co-ordinate execution of the plan at the national, state, conurbation and municipal levels, but it fell to another ministry (Programming and Budgeting – SPP) to *promote* it. This dependence upon the goodwill and support of another sector was a major stumbling block. Moreover, the National Urban Development Plan was further dependent upon the goodwill of other sectors if it was to be operative. Particularly important was the attitude adopted by the Ministry for the Promotion of Industry (SEPAFIN) whose National Industrial Development Plan, although ostensibly congruent with the National Urban Development Plan, in fact added a further 16 priority areas to the 11 zones already established, and in effect rendered SAHOP's initiative virtually inoperable. Despite its apparent 'activity', planning remained passive in so far as it followed the pattern established by the so-called 'efficient' sectors of economic growth (Unikel & Lavell 1979). It therefore validated the economic imperatives of the day.

The traditional dominance of economic over physical planning has been reasserted by President De la Madrid. Although a 'technocrat', his background was firmly set in economics, and while he was Minister of SPP there was little love lost between his group and the physical planning axis in SAHOP and in the DDF. The result has been a downgrading of physical planning since 1983. SAHOP was emasculated: the large slice of its resources represented by public works was removed, and it was renamed the Secretariat of Urban Development and Ecology (SEDUE).[7]

The same shifts in the importance and impact of planning are to be observed in the context of urban planning for Mexico City. Although a planning structure had been in existence since 1938 and was quite active in the 1930s and 1940s, it had lapsed under the influence of Mayor Uruchurtu (1952–66), for whom 'planning was alien to the spirit and methods of . . . operation, which stressed secrecy, flexible interpretation of laws and regulations, rapidity, and spectacular short-term results' (Fried 1972: 680).

Echeverría's administration established the groundwork for the emergence of a fully fledged city planning system that took place between 1980–83. For the first time (1972) an independent Planning Directorate was created responsible to the Federal District Secretariat of Public Works. It was charged with developing the Master Plan, and with planning and zoning. Late in the same *sexenio* the Federal District Urban Development Law was passed which made mandatory the existence of a City Plan, with subplans to cover each *delegacíon*. In addition the urban area was to have a proper zoning system. Despite these initiatives no planning system was in operation until the end of the decade, when Mayor Hank González implemented a Federal District Master Plan, together with *delegación* subplans (both in 1980) and a zoning law (1982).

I have described the details of this plan and the process of its acceptance elsewhere (Ward 1981b), and do not wish to repeat them here. Suffice to say that not only was a technically competent plan implemented for the first time, but an institutionalized apparatus was created to exercise planning controls over city growth and building activity. Mexico City, for a short spell at least, moved from a period of paper *plans* to a process of *planning*. Unfortunately, many of these initiatives have lost impetus or been quashed since 1983. Paralleling the shift away from physical towards economic planning at the national level, Mexico City's incipient urban planning process has been placed on the back burner. Although a new Federal District Secretariat for Planning has been created and has strong political backing from Mayor Ramón Aquirre, its primary concern is with the Federal District's contribution to the (economic) National Development Plan. Physical planning, such as it is, remains the responsibility of a politically weak Federal District Secretariat for Urban Development and Ecology.[8]

Thus there are indications that in the late 1970s and early 1980s planning functioned much more systematically and effectively than ever before. But as I shall argue below, there were good reasons that account for these changes which suggest that planning is highly functional to the maintenance of the Mexican political system.

The rationale of planning
The way in which planning is administered both nationally and locally offers clear political advantages for contemporary Mexican governments. Although Figure 3.1 is not exhaustive of all departments which include certain planning functions within the city (the water agency and transport commission are omitted, for example), it indicates quite clearly the difficulty that any single agency has in exercising *authority* over the planning process.[9] There is an obvious multiplicity of offices with responsibility for planning. In part this may be explained by the existence of two federal entities across which the city sprawls. But it also reflects the political tradition for incoming administrations

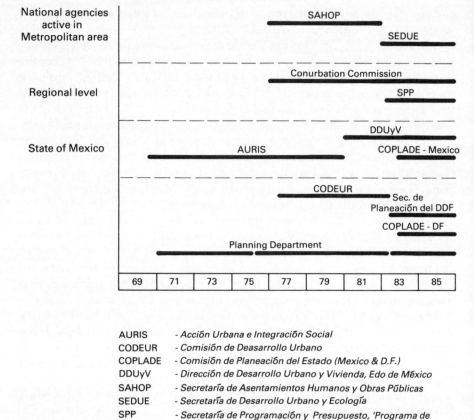

Figure 3.1 Departments and agencies with responsibilities for urban planning in Mexico City, 1970–85. The Federal District planning department has changed its name from the Dirección General de Planificación to Planeación, to Desarrollo Urbano y Vivienda, to Desarrollo Urbano.

to create new departments to compete with, or to take over, some of the duties of those already in existence. This acts to enhance the opportunities for patronage by providing jobs within the bureaucracy. It also allows the Executive and Mayor to manipulate and play off one political faction against another. Despite the fact that the most recent administration sets great store by administrative efficiency, it is quite clear that there has been a proliferation of the bureaucracy with responsibilities for planning in Mexico City since 1982.

Another notable point in Figure 3.1 is the fact that the government has never sought to create an effective city-wide planning authority. The Conurbation Commission does not fulfil this role but is an advisory body at a much larger scale, covering five central states and the Federal District. Nor does the more recently established Programme for the Metropolitan Region (a department in SPP), which is pitched at a regional scale and is a broad normative document with no executive status. The COPLADES, too, are committees with a broad representative base designed to stimulate local participation of the public and private sectors in economic development, rather than to act as an executive body for physical planning.

Thus for city planning to begin to be effective requires close collaboration between the principal planning agencies on either side of the Federal District boundary. Co-operation of this nature is unlikely, given that personnel invariably form part of different *camarillas* and that competition between bureaucratic factions is the hallmark of the Mexican governmental system. A recent example is the formulation of SPP's metropolitan programme which was elaborated *without* consultation and input from SEDUE, the Conurbation Commission, or the Urban Development Departments in the State of Mexico and the Federal District.[10]

Another way in which the promotion of planning in the Federal District served a useful political function is demonstrated by Mayor Hank González's adoption of it during the late 1970s. Prior to that time the planning directorate was extremely 'lightweight' politically and was always susceptible to being ignored or overruled by the big spending and more powerful departments which resented its co-ordinating functions. It is perhaps a little ironic that planning was implemented under a mayor who personally had little sympathy or interest in it when he took office in 1977. Rather, his concern was to engage in major construction works that offered opportunities for disbursing patronage and for self-enrichment. Yet he realized that a Master Plan offered several advantages. First, it complied with the law which demanded the existence and regular review of a Master Plan. However, by itself this is an inadequate explanation: it would have been quite easy to produce a flimsy plan or a suitable revision of an earlier Plan that had been presented (but not implemented) in 1976. Indeed, for the first 18 months the mayor kept the earlier plan 'on ice' and showed little inclination to revise or implement it.

Secondly, the mayor required support in his fight for extra resources to carry out the building programme already underway. This certainly prompted his initial return to the idea of updating the 1976 Plan. During 1978–9 there was an enormous increase in expenditure undertaken by the public works department and by COVITUR. Opposition to these building programmes was encountered within Cabinet and also on the streets, where protest had erupted against the destruction of tree-lined avenues and the eviction of residents due to street widening associated with the construction of the urban highways (*ejes viales*). The mayor needed to be able to demonstrate that these programmes were properly thought through and integrated within the Master Plan. Thus the plan required speedy elaboration and for political reasons it was entrusted to SAHOP.[11]

A third reason for planning implementation around this time was the fact that traditional forms of mediation were no longer adequate. Patron–client links which had predominated between high-ranking government officials and local communities were replaced from 1977 onwards by a more formal arrangement of state–community relations embodied within the *juntas de vecinos* structure (see Ward 1981a, and Chapter 5 below). As part of this change the planning system began to be used to provide political legitimacy. This became imperative once the level of debate over urban issues had begun to be more informed. Interest in urbanism was no longer a preserve of elitist and relatively conservative groups such as the Architects' and Engineers' Professional Societies, nor was it an academic backwater: it had entered the mainstream of politics. For several years a radical school of architecture (*Autogibierno*) at the National University had trained graduates with a very different perspective about urban development, which challenged conventional approaches. More-over, several other professional courses had emerged such as the Human Settlements degree at the Metropolitan University. More significantly, per-haps, was the concerted and informed criticism that had begun regularly to enter the press, many of whose columnists were lecturing staff on those courses. Others were advisers to left-wing political parties which were beginning to flex their muscles after the political reforms of 1973 and 1978. Information and critical argument entered party manifestos and even Congress through minority party representatives. An organization called CONAMUP, which had success-fully welded a large number of low-income settlements into a united body, was beginning to assert itself as a national force by 1980 and was very active within the capital. There was, therefore, a growing sophistication of argument about urban development which demanded sound technical answers that could only be provided by a competent planning team. A dynamic planning system now became an important tool for political mediation.

Fourthly, planning suits a variety of interest groups within society. As we have observed, it suits government in so far as planning legitimizes decisions. The principal motive for revising the Master Plan was to incorporate the new urban highway system and the extensions to the Metro, both of which had been decided on behind closed doors by the mayor and his intimates without consultation with the planning department or the public. The Plan in existence now provides further legitimacy to justify decisions to evict squatters and other groups from newly formed irregular settlements. Elsewhere it may justify decisions not to extend services. Ideologically, too, the planning department strengthens the ability of the government to meet criticisms about its handling of urban development problems.

Land developers and speculators may be affected negatively in so far as they no longer have a free hand to develop what they want where they want. They will be obliged to comply with the more rigorous regulations that now exist. If they do not then their developments may be closed down. However, they also benefit in that the Plan offers an amnesty and effectively condones previous illegal transactions they may have made. Moreover, the incorporation of land and land uses into the plan that were previously excluded is likely to raise land values in the affected areas.

For the general public the outcome is mixed. Middle-income groups are more likely to adhere to zoning regulations and to seek formal planning permissions as they have neither the resources nor the political weight to overcome planning regulations. However, they may be expected to gain in that they are able to press more strongly for the exclusion of any undesirable land use from their neighbourhood. Low-income housebuilders are unlikely to seek full planning permissions, but they may benefit where their previously unrecognized settlement is included on the plan and in the zoning. This enhances their security of tenure and may strengthen their claim for service provision. But it may also work the opposite way by isolating those settlements that fall beyond the servicing grid and justify their eradication.

However, the adoption of a formal planning system entailed certain undesirable trade-offs for the government. Inevitably it would add further to the dissemination of information about Mexico City's urban development. It also required some curtailment of particularistic decisions by *delegados* such as issuing their friends with planning permissions for developments that were not authorized by the Plan. Run-of-the-mill decisions were now much more likely to be decided on technical criteria rather than political ones. But, for the government, these were relatively small concessions to make, and in any case they were probably inevitable once the level of public debate had risen.

Clearly the apparent rejection of physical planning from 1983 might at first sight contradict my argument that planning departments will play an increasing role in political management. In some of my most recent interviews with high-ranking functionaries I attempted to explore this point. Some officials expressed surprise that an urban planning department had survived *at all*. Given that the emphasis of the president and Mayor Aguirre was on economic planning and administrative efficiency, and given their personal antipathy towards many of the leading figures associated with the physical planning under the previous administration, it was suggested that the continued existence of an 'urban development' department was unexpected. Yet it survived in a very weakened state, and its previous chief was confirmed in his post. The only explanations are either administrative ineptitude or, more likely, that some form of physical planning structure remains politically useful. It saves formally changing the law to revoke the Master Plan, with all the political embarrassment that would cause. It provides an important cushion for politicians to meet public criticism when urban infrastructure fails, as occurred when there was intense flooding during the 1984 rainy season. A planning programme also gives the illusion of activity and may be used to head off social unrest. In Mayor Aguirre's own words when presenting the revised 'plan' in 1984: 'the Government of the

Federal District cannot allow things to continue on their present course, and cannot allow such an important problem for the maintenance of social stability to get out of hand' (*Ovaciones* 24 September 1984). Although physical planning is low priority, its survival in vestige form is politically useful.

Public participation in planning
In many respects public participation is the acid test of whether a true process of planning exists or not. Several high-level planning officials in Mexico singled it out as the most important criterion in any definition of planning. They saw it as a means of ensuring that planning policy was carried out. By incorporating the public into the process and making them aware of the issues at stake and of public authorities' obligation to install and maintain essential services, planners sought to establish a dynamic whereby proposals contained within the Master Plan would be implemented. Similarly a raised level of public consciousness might help sustain policies across *sexenios* and provide a degree of continuity previously lacking in the Mexican political system. However, these statements suggest a greater concern for information dissemination rather than public *participation* in decision making or in the effective ordering of local priorities. Even planning officials most sympathetic to the idea of public participation demonstrated little understanding about how the public might actively be involved.

Since 1983 the term 'participation' has also been widely emphasized by De la Madrid. First a series of 'Popular Consultations' have been established to feed in ideas and opinions to inform government policy. Although these meetings have generated substantial involvement from a wide range of interest groups, there is little evidence that proposals have been taken on board. Secondly, in May 1983 a National Democratic Planning System was established under the aegis of SPP. Its functions cover the organization of 'popular consultations' and specific forums such as municipal reform; to make proposals for the implementation of state-wide planning systems; to create regional plans; to assist the implementation of the National Development Plan; to co-ordinate the President's State of the Nation report and so on (Mexico SPP 1983: xviv). There is little in either of the two structures to suggest genuine participation: at best they are consultative, and at worst they are channels for the dissemination of information on behalf of government.

Therefore public participation in the planning process in Mexico is more nominal than real. In many ways the failure to incorporate a far higher level of active and real public involvement constitutes the most important single caveat to the argument that a planning system has been introduced in Mexico City. Moreover, it is difficult to envisage greater devolution of decision making to local groups occurring in the immediate or medium-term future. Planning may persist, and structures designed to facilitate community–state interaction and popular participation may continue to evolve, but their *raison d'être* will be one of maintaining the status quo. Genuine innovations to give power to local organizations will require fundamental societal and political changes. The shifts that we have observed in this chapter have been superficial rather than fundamental. Nevertheless they are important, and I suggest that they are probably the outcome more of a technocratic commitment to economic growth and to the consequent need for efficient management, than a genuine political commitment to improve the welfare of the poor. We are now in a position to explore this proposition further, and in the remaining chapters I analyse government performance and purpose in the context of land development for low-income housing, servicing poor communities, and the provision of health care.

Notes

1 An attempt to 'democratize' the inner workings of the party had been made by its president Carlos Madrazo early during the Díaz Ordaz administration (1964–70). He attempted to instil greater rank-and-file participation in party life, thereby threatening to reduce the influence of regional and sectoral bosses. This encountered strong resistance and he was quickly replaced. His subsequent death when a light airplane in which he was travelling crashed over Acapulco Bay has prompted speculation that he might have been assassinated.

2 In the past the importance of high-ranking officials appearing before a Senate Committee for confirmation was nominal. However, the process has been revitalized by De la Madrid and in 1982–3, Senate interrogation of appointees was more vigorous than ever before. It was also widely publicized.

3 To a certain extent, therefore, López Portillo is right to argue that the *técnico* versus *político* split is an artificial one (quoted in Needler 1982: 82). However, lower levels of government bureaucracy do appear to be run increasingly along technocratic lines.

4 Where individuals are sufficiently powerful to threaten the president then it is not uncommon for them to be given an ambassadorship to remove them physically from the mainstream of political life.

5 These definitions are not my own but were identified in earlier joint work with Alan Gilbert. Readers may wish to consult the original text for a more detailed discussion of the literature (Gilbert & Ward 1985).

6 For example, the River Basin Programmes in Mexico (1947), the Autonomous Corporation for the Cauca Valley in Colombia (1954), the Brazilian Superintendency for the Development of the North East (SUDENE, in 1959), and the Venezuelan Corporation for Guayana established in 1958 (see Gilbert 1974: 238, Stohr 1972). Urban planning, if it was considered at all, was relegated to become a subset of these broader projects – such as the group responsible for planning the new city of Ciudad Guayana (Rodwin *et al.* 1969).

7 Given SEDUE's lack of political weight in the De la Madrid administration it is not particularly surprising that it has achieved little. Since 1983 there has only been one 'Plan', the president's National Development Plan, 1983–8. All other initiatives are termed 'programmes', and in 1984 SEDUE published a National Urban and Housing Programme which is little more than a watered-down and less ambitious version of the previous (1978) urban development plan.

8 In fact *both* of these secretariats were abolished in July/August 1985 as part of the public sector cut backs initiated at that time. The General Directorate of Planning remains, however.

9 In the Federal District the department responsible is the Directorate of Planning (though the name changed in 1983); while in the State of Mexico it was AURIS until 1982, and since then the State General Directorate of Urban Development and Housing has had primary responsibility.

10   A further reason for low levels of collaboration is that it is unlikely that two planning
     departments at any one time will have roughly equal status. The influence of one group is likely
     to be waxing or waning with respect to the other. It would be a magnanimous gesture for that
     department which was on the 'up' to assist its less fortunate counterpart. Therefore, at best one
     is likely to find little more than active communication between departments; at worst each will
     attempt to undercut the initiatives of the other. The post-1981 evidence of more active informal
     collaboration between the Planning Department of the Federal District and the Directorate of
     Urban Development and Housing in the State of Mexico is the exception that proves the rule.
     Both 'teams' emerged from the same group of one directorate in SAHOP and were, therefore,
     ex-colleagues and often personal friends.

11   We can only speculate about the reasons for this rather unprecedented request to another
     ministry to prepare the Federal District Plan. It may have been prompted by the continuance in
     office of a planning chief whom the mayor did not trust, but in the event when she was
     eventually replaced responsibility for the Plan remained primarily with SAHOP. Undoubtedly
     an important consideration was the close political alliance between personnel in DDF and in
     SAHOP. For a fuller discussion see Ward (1981b: 56–7).

4   Land provision: an effective housing policy?

Public housing programmes in Latin America rarely reach the majority of the population either because insufficient dwellings are constructed or because the poor cannot afford those that are built. Although the creation of large housing funds such as BNH in Brazil and INFONAVIT in Mexico played an important role in increasing the quantity of dwellings during the 1970s, supply remains grossly inadequate (COPEVI 1977a, Garza & Schteingart 1978). Thus for the majority of the poor who are obliged to resort to self-build house construction, land policy is, in effect, the housing policy.

Proper understanding of the land market, how it functions, the nature of private and public intervention and the impact that this has upon land prices and housing tenure are crucially important. Yet until very recently in Latin American social science, there were relatively few specific analyses of the issue of land market behaviour: most studies treated it as an important but secondary matter in the investigation of irregular settlement. Nevertheless interest in the land issue has quickened since the beginning of the 1980s. The processes of land alienation to create irregular settlement and the reasons for differences observed between countries have begun to be discussed in detail (Gilbert 1981a), as have the ways in which this enhances capital accumulation for different agents involved in the process (Pradilla 1976, Schteingart 1981). Governments, too, are turning their attention towards the land market as they adopt a position of direct involvement in the sphere of land development through mechanisms such as sites and services, land readjustment, advance acquisition, land assembly, betterment taxation, and the use of windfall gains to cross-subsidize or finance low-cost housing development (Shroup 1978, Ward 1981c, Doebele 1983, Devas 1983). Governments are also seeking greater control over the 'upgrading' and improvement process in existing settlements (Payne 1984, Skinner & Rodell 1983, Angel 1983b). There is widespread debate about whether or not the impact of this intervention is beneficial to low-income groups (Ward 1982c, Gilbert 1984). Does it lead to a substantial development of the housing stock, wider investment in fixed assets, and to the improvement of urban living conditions (Linn 1983)? Or does it open up the 'informal sector' to the process of capital accumulation, thereby driving up housing costs, intensifying exploitation through extensions to the working day, and so inducing a decline in living standards (Burgess 1982)? But if the existence of irregular settlement in its various forms is functional for capital in cheapening the cost of reproduction of labour power, why did it take so long for self-help to gain public acceptability (Peattie 1979, Gilbert & Gugler 1982)?

If informal processes of land supply have, in the past, proved quite successful in providing widespread opportunities for land acquisition by the poor, then there is a recent current of opinion which argues that this is breaking down (Ward 1982a, Angel *et al.* 1983). It has been argued that there is a growing tendency for large commercial enterprises to take over the forms of land supply previously dominated by small-scale, informal agents. This intervention is being assisted wittingly or unwittingly by government practice (Baross 1983, Durand-Lasserve 1983). Land prices have become too expensive and are no longer affordable to the same proportion of the population as before (Evers 1977, Carroll 1980). But as we shall observe in this chapter the evidence for this argument is inconclusive.

Finally, there is a growing awareness that it might prove fruitful to consider traditional rights of land holding that already exist in many countries and to try to adapt them in contemporary urban planning. Community land, use-rights, customary land, and other forms may provide a much more sensitive and widely understood basis for land occupancy than, say, those provided under the provisions of existing norms and laws (Lea 1983, Varley 1985, Crooke 1983). Ingenious hybrids of these traditional practices might be encouraged to good effect (Turnbull 1983). Obviously it is impossible to broach more than a few of these issues in the course of this chapter. Those that I select should not necessarily be construed as the most important. Rather they reflect those that I have encountered given my research methodology, and my wish to examine urban land development in the context of the Mexican political system.

Methods of land acquisition for irregular settlement in Latin America

In any society the process of land allocation is highly competitive between groups. There has to be some mechanism by which particular groups gain priority over certain areas of land before others. In most capitalist societies it is the market which acts to allocate land: those who can afford to pay more, or according to economic theory are less indifferent to location, acquire the more desirable areas (Gilbert & Ward 1985). In Mexico City, as we shall observe below, the vast majority of the poor are at the bottom end of a single market and the land that they bid for is cheap because full title is not provided, and it is unserviced, poorly located, and undesired by economically better-off groups. To that extent they may be said to hold a monopoly over the land at the outset, but the process of commercial exchange penetrates this market very soon afterwards.

There are innumerable ways in which the poor acquire land, within the broad generalization that they are usually illegal (Leeds 1969). Basically, however, there are two alternatives open: the first is to invade land and the second is to purchase land beyond the limits of the conventional, legalized housing areas (Gilbert & Ward 1985).[1] At particular times invasions have been the main form of land acquisition in Lima (Turner 1969, Collier 1976, Dietz 1977, 1980), in most Venezuelan cities (Ray 1969), in Rio de Janeiro during the 1950s and early 1960s (Leeds & Leeds 1976), and in Chile between 1969 and 1973 (Cleaves 1974, Kusnetzoff 1975, Lozano 1975). By contrast, land invasions have generally not been permitted in Bogotá (Vernez 1973, Doebele 1975), or in Rio de Janeiro after 1964 (Valladares 1978, Portes 1979). In Mexico City they occurred most frequently during the 1950s and 1960s when there was a ban on low-income subdivisions within the Federal District, although their formation during this period was usually gradual and accretive. Large-scale invasions were more common after Mayor Uruchurtu lost office in 1966 and during the earlier years of the Echeverría administration when the political climate encouraged popular mobilization – points to which I return later.

The purchase of land may also take many forms and is common throughout Latin America. In Mexico City it is by far the most important means whereby the poor get land. One way in which land is acquired is through company-sponsored illegal subdivisions (*fraccionamientos clandestinos*) in which title is usually provided but services are few and far between. The scale of these developments sets them apart from other Latin American, or indeed from most other Mexican subdivisions. Settlements comprising several thousand families are common in Netzahualcóyotl and Ecatepec (Fig. 4.1). Alternatively, plots are purchased on *ejidal* (community) lands, and this is the most significant form of land acquisition. An estimated 16% of the total city population in 1970 was living on land that was *ejidal* in origin (Varley 1985, COPEVI 1977a, and Fig. 4.1.). The sale of plots – again without services – takes place either directly by individual *ejidatarios*, or by their elected local representatives – the *comisariado ejidal* (Mexico SAHOP 1979, Connolly 1982, Varley 1985). Whichever applies, the process is illegal because *ejidatarios* have use-rights only over the land which is, theoretically, inalienable. Nor is it only low-income groups that are involved: during the 1960s large tracts of *ejidal* land were privatized for elite housing developments, while in the 1970s rich and poor alike bought plots illegally on *ejidal* lands in the south of the city (COPEVI 1977b, Varley 1985). Today the largest single area of active low-income settlement formation is on the far eastern frontier of Mexico City on the *ejido* of Ayotla, which extends over some 2500 hectares.

The general tolerance of illegality with respect to low-income housing in Latin American cities is not incidental to the survival of the Latin American state: it serves a wide variety of interests (Gilbert & Ward 1985). My argument is that in Mexico illegality of land holdings and the response of different governments can only be understood in the context of political mediation and social control. By 'political mediation' I mean the ways in which the state attempts to advance the interests of powerful and organized groups which it seeks to placate, and at the same time manages to maintain social control and to legitimate itself through the securement of political support for the govern-ment. I also hope to show that the poor have benefited despite consistent state

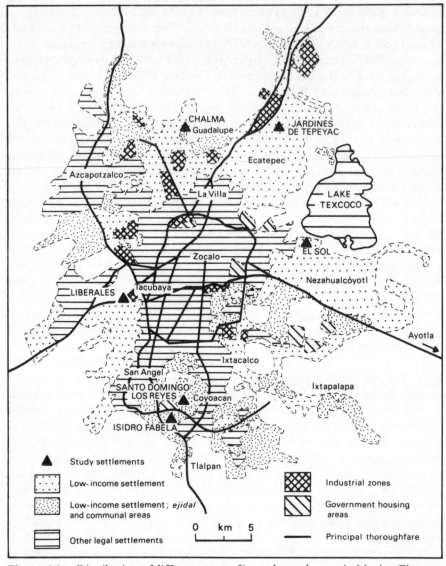

Figure 4.1.   Distribution of different types of irregular settlement in Mexico City.

action in favour of other social groups. Through land invasion and illegal subdivision some of the poor receive land upon which they can consolidate their homes. Low-income settlement provides them with a base from which they can seek work, raise their families and usually improve their absolute standards of living. For 'owner–occupiers' the plot of land comprises an increasingly valuable asset and although conditions in which they live are usually hostile and rarely conducive to a comfortable existence, comparison with rural conditions or with the lives of some low-income renters normally recommends their situation. Despite the poor living conditions illegal settlements act as a safety valve to social tension. As such, only where conditions deteriorate markedly is there any likelihood of the poor reacting politically *en masse*.

Changing government response to irregular settlement

An analysis of government intervention in the land market must take account of both *action* and *inaction* on the part of the authorities. Failure to act may reflect policy choices and this has been (and continues to be) an important feature of Mexico's management of low-income land developments. In order to understand government policy since 1970 it is important to look at events prior to the Echeverría administration, as the large proportion of contemporary irregular settlement was formed before that date and affords important insights into the nature and rationale of state response. Two types of response are identified: first, those actions that affected the *provision* of land for low-income settlement, and secondly *remedial actions* such as regularization, recognition and approval to extend services to unregularized areas.

Land for housing the poor: the laissez-faire *period prior to 1970*
The first *colonias populares* emerged in the 1920s in the north and east of the city centre (Sudra 1976, Perló 1979). Rapid population growth brought about by industrialization during the 1930s and 1940s was accommodated in rental tenements in the inner city and by the early expansion of the *colonias*. Indeed, by 1952 14% of the city population was already estimated to live in self-build housing in irregular settlements in the Federal District. These settlements accounted for 24% of the built-up area at the time (Mexico BNH 1952, Ward 1976a). In 1970 the population in the *colonias populares* had risen to around 4.5 million, or just over 50% of the city total and between 40% and 50% of the built-up area (COPEVI 1977a, Ward 1976a). Effectively, during the intervening 20 years the housing structure of Mexico City was decided, both within the Federal District and in surrounding municipalities. Much of the post-1970 growth has comprised infilling and densification of these recently formed areas, though there has also been significant expansion, particularly in the State of Mexico. In 1984 an estimated 8 or 9 million inhabitants lived in *colonias populares*, though obviously regularization of many areas has meant that they are no longer illegal; nor are many residents pioneer 'self-builders', but recent arrivals to the settlement, many of whom rent rooms or share land with kinsmen.

Government policy towards the provision of land for low-income housing between 1950 and 1970 differed on either side of the Federal District boundary. Within the boundary a firm attempt was made to prevent its expansion. There is little doubt that this is directly the result of the influence of Mayor Uruchurtu, who successfully imposed a ban on planning approval for new low-income subdivisions between 1953 and 1966 (Cornelius 1975). This does not mean that no new settlements were created: many developed on vacant land for which approval had already been granted. Aerial photographs for the eastern suburbs of the city around the airport in 1952 show quite clearly that extensive areas of land were subdivided ready for sale. Elsewhere, landlords who found that they could not openly develop low-income settlements turned a blind eye to invasions of their land or rented out plots informally (Mexico INVI 1958). Some *ejidatarios* were able to sell their land to the poor because the DDF had no jurisdiction over the transactions. Only when approval was sought to extend services to settlements on *ejidal* land could Uruchurtu exercise his authority and withhold permission – as when he blocked a request for a mixed lower- and middle-income subdivision in Padierna in 1959–60 (Durand 1983, and Padierna archive in Agrarian Reform Ministry SRA).

At first sight this concerted attempt to control and prevent land provision for the poor within the Federal District seems to contradict my earlier argument that irregular settlement is functional to the interests of the state. Yet it appears to have been the result of Uruchurtu's concern to prevent what he saw as sprawling shanty-town development and the burden that servicing these settlements would impose on the Treasury. Certainly that is how he justified his actions. However, that he was allowed to pursue the policy may be explained by the absence, within the Federal District, of a powerful and co-ordinated group of low-income land developers; by the 'safety valve' offered by the expansion of settlement in the adjacent municipalities of the State of Mexico; and, lastly, by the opportunities for settlement within the Federal District on *ejidal* land and on lands for which permissions had already been granted. Significantly, opposition to Uruchurtu began to increase in the 1960s after his consistent refusal to extend services to many low-income settlements and, perhaps more importantly, once his policies began to threaten the more powerful groups involved in speculative land development in the south of the city (López Díaz 1978). That his policies had become dysfunctional to the state by 1966 when he was forced from office is also suggested by the more circumspect and conciliatory approach of his successors (Cornelius 1975, Alonso *et al.* 1980).

No direct attempt was made by either the Federal District or by the State of Mexico government to use *ejidal* land for low-income housing purposes, despite the clear opportunity that it provided. One author, as early as 1965, noted: 'Land reserves of this kind, under public control, have long been advocated in many metropolitan areas, but few can match the good fortune of Mexico City in having such reserves readily at hand' (Frieden 1965: 86). Good fortune or not, the government failed to act.

In the State of Mexico during the 1950s and 1960s the authorities acted consistently to further the interests of the land developers.[2] The Improvement Boards established by the governor from 1952 onwards, ostensibly to co-ordinate the installation of services in the region, achieved little beyond the promotion of lot sales on behalf of the companies. My interviews with leaders in Jardines de Tepeyac in Ecatepec revealed that local municipal officers were in the pay of the company responsible for the subdivision. Moreover, the State authorities took no action against the common abuse whereby the same plot was sold several times over to different individuals. Nor did they attempt to disguise their support for the companies, even when many settlers formed themselves into 'defence associations' and demanded that promises of service installation be upheld (Guerrero *et al.* 1974). Despite comprehensive regulations governing the creation of low-income sub-divisions (the *Ley de fraccionamientos* of 1958), neither the State nor the Federal Government pressed for sanctions against the developers. Rather, until 1969, authorizations for further developments continued to be given by the authorities even where the offending companies had failed to satisfy the conditions laid down in earlier settlements (Guerrero *et al.* 1974, Connolly 1982). Although there is little evidence of direct overlap of personnel between company and government officials it seems certain that graft and other 'kickbacks' played an important part in keeping government well disposed towards illegal developers. Not until the 1970s was any serious attempt made to penalize the developers. This was a consequence of the complicity between the State authorities and the companies throughout most of the period.

The supply of land through *ejidos* was also assisted by government action and inaction throughout this period. Legally the use of *ejidal* land for urban expansion is prohibited under the Agrarian Law (Article 91). However, *ejidal* land may be disestablished 'in the public interest' in either one of two ways: by *permuta* or exchange of one area of *ejido* for equivalent lands elsewhere; or by expropriation. There was widespread abuse of *permutas* during the 1950s and 1960s to secure land for a variety of purposes, not all of which can be justified as having been in the public interest. Large upper-income residential districts such as Jardines de Pedregal and part of Ciudad Satélite came into being in this manner (COPEVI 1977b). Low-income irregular settlement was usually formed through the manipulation of a legal facility whereby part of an *ejido* may be set aside as an 'urban centre' to house the *ejidatarios* and other community workers. Application would be made to the Agrarian Reform Department for an urban *ejidal* zone, or for the extension of an existing one, but meanwhile lots would be 'sold' by the *ejidal* community. The formal procedure to create an urban zone on an *ejido* is a long and complicated one, and often the later stages are never reached because after several years the settlement is a *fait accompli*. It then becomes a matter for regularization (Varley 1985).

Remedial actions on the part of the state were limited before 1970 on both sides of the Federal District boundary. Within the District regularization of selected settlements occurred either through persuading the landlord to install services and to give legal title, or more usually by expropriation and resale to residents. In theory there was an agreement between the Electricity Company and the DDF that current would not be installed until legal title had been obtained; in practice supply was often provided.

The provision of standpipes, regularization, and lightweight one-off campaigns to vaccinate children, or to remove rubbish from settlements, were negotiated by the Oficina de Colonias in the Federal District and by the municipal authorities in the State of Mexico. In both cases the PRI, particularly through its CNOP wing, was heavily involved as mediator between residents and the government (Cornelius 1975, Eckstein 1977, Alonso et al. 1980). Government response appears to have been more sympathetic to irregular settlements after Uruchurtu's resignation in 1966 (Cornelius 1975). In the Federal District, land regularization and service provision began to assume importance as a means of ensuring and developing political control and support. Through the Oficina de Colonias residents were mobilized to attend political rallies and to vote for the PRI at elections; in exchange they could expect some form of government recognition for their settlement, and/or the installation of minor services and occasional handouts.[3] This process of negotiation was mediated vertically through settlement leaders who acted as 'brokers' in informal patron–client networks involving the community and top-level politicians and government officials (Cornelius 1973, 1975).

By and large this practice worked well for the authorities in the Federal District and was extended once Echeverría took office. However, the same success was not achieved in the State of Mexico, where a major political crisis was about to break. Population in Netzahualcóyotl alone had grown to over 600 000 by 1970; the area was almost devoid of services and the residents' associations had begun to mobilize and organize themselves *horizontally* into a single organization.[4] The friendly Frankenstein's monster created by the companies now threatened to run amok, generating social unrest and political protest. Government response is illuminating.

Land for housing the poor: the interventionist period, 1971–6
This crisis in the State of Mexico prompted a much more interventionist approach in the handling of the land issue, especially in the area of remedial action which was tackled in several ways (Tello 1978, Ward 1981a). Firstly, the new administration was faced with an acute political dilemma. The mass-based organization in Netzahualcóyotl (Movimiento Restaurador de Colonos – the MRC) had called a strike on further payments to the land developers, and both residents and the companies turned to the government to resolve the question in their favour. Residents protested that they had been overcharged for poor quality land and that services promised by developers had never arrived. The companies wanted the money still owed them. The solution was a highly political one. A trust fund (Fideicomiso Netzahualcóyotl – FINEZA) was established in which the companies were to receive the sums owed to them less 40%, while the residents were to get a 15% discount on the overall purchase price, and to receive from government full legal title to their lots. Service

installation would begin immediately, also provided by the government, but the costs were to be recovered from residents over a ten-year period. The agreement was accepted by all parties, though it has been strongly criticized for favouring the companies in so far as they were exonerated from responsibility for their illegal transactions, retained a large part of their profits, and escaped the burden of paying for services (Guerrero *et al*. 1974, Martín de la Rosa 1975, Ferras 1978).

The second way in which the Echeverría administration adopted a more interventionist stance was to create a host of agencies and institutions with responsibility for irregular settlements (Tello 1978, Ward 1981a). Several features of the structure and functioning of this newly created bureaucracy show how the covert aims of maintaining social control and of facilitating political mediation were more important than the efficient exercise of land regularization and housing improvement. Most of these agencies fall quite clearly at the 'political' end of the spectrum outlined in Chapter 3.

For instance, the multiplicity of agencies created with regularization duties within the Metropolitan Area (Fig. 4.2) suggests enormous overlaps of duties similar to those which we identified for planning in the previous chapter. CoRett's charter gave it responsibility for *ejidal* and *comunal* lands. But, in the State of Mexico, AURIS was also involved in *ejidal* land. During the last days of the Díaz Ordaz administration officials had rushed through the expropriation of an enormous area of *ejidal* and given AURIS the responsibility of regularizing and commercializing these lands for 'social interest' housing purposes. Similarly in the Federal District, FIDEURBE was created specifically for the task of regularizing the most conflictive settlements (including Padierna and Santo Domingo), and many of these were on *ejidal* or *comunal* lands. An added problem was that responsibility for several of these settlements had rested initially with INDECO so there was likely to be an overlap of functions and channels of communication between the agency and different community leaders brought about by the transfer of responsibility from the first agency to its successor. INDECO was an agency with a broad range of functions, which meant that it operated nationally as a sort of roving 'troubleshooter' and was charged to resolve problems in specific settlements as and when they arose. A classic example was its intervention in Colonia Ruben Jaramillo in Cuernavaca, which had developed on what were originally *ejidal* lands though they had been 'acquired' by kinsmen of the governor (Montaño 1976: 184). The Procuraduría de Colonias Populares (PCP) had a similarly vague role to fulfil within the Federal District. It was the old Oficina de Colonias reconstituted by Mayor Sentíes to act as a vehicle whereby he could intervene in low-income settlement affairs. It had some regularization duties but also distributed free milk, gave out presents to children at Christmas, organized clear-up campaigns and so on. The *procurador* saw himself, literally, as the advocate of the poor.

A further indication of the 'political' nature of several of these agencies is provided by their very low budgets and the constant insecurity about financial

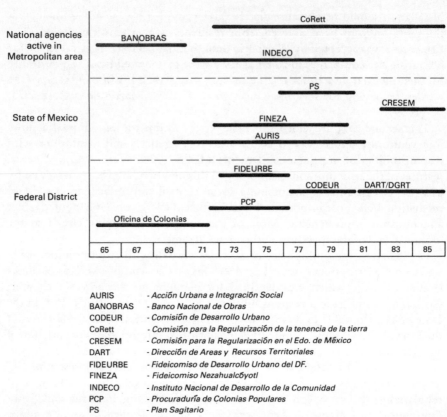

	AURIS	- *Acción Urbana e Integración Social*
	BANOBRAS	- *Banco Nacional de Obras*
	CODEUR	- *Comisión de Desarrollo Urbano*
	CoRett	- *Comisión para la Regularización de la tenencia de la tierra*
	CRESEM	- *Comisión para la Regularización en el Edo. de México*
	DART	- *Dirección de Areas y Recursos Territoriales*
	FIDEURBE	- *Fideicomiso de Desarrollo Urbano del DF.*
	FINEZA	- *Fideicomiso Nezahualcóyotl*
	INDECO	- *Instituto Nacional de Desarrollo de la Comunidad*
	PCP	- *Procuraduría de Colonias Populares*
	PS	- *Plan Sagitario*

Figure 4.2 Departments and agencies with responsibilities for land regularization in Mexico City, 1965–85.

resources. This applies less in the case of AURIS, which was established in 1970 with 20 million pesos 'seed' capital and was expected to be self-financing thereafter. Careful commercialization of its land reserves allowed it to thrive. However, several of the other agencies had low budgets which barely covered their administrative costs and which fluctuated widely from one year to the next. Indeed FIDEURBE, despite being a 'brainchild' of Echeverría, had major financial problems from the outset. Established with an initial 3 million peso bridging loan, its request for a further loan of 60 million pesos in 1973, although supported by the presidencia, was thwarted for several months by the Treasury which argued that funds should derive from the Federal District's overall budget. The matter was only resolved by executive intervention from the presidency.

Inter-agency strife is another feature of the bureaucratic structure and political mediation. As in the case for planning, the informal 'rules' governing interdepartmental functioning at all hierarchical levels are, broadly, those of either outright conflict and competition, alliance, or tacit agreement not to meddle in each other's affairs. Of these three alternatives, 'alliance' did not figure during this period in relations between the agencies depicted in Figure 4.2. However, between 1973 and 1976 there is ample evidence from my own fieldwork and that of others that both FIDEURBE and the PCP suffered from, and engendered conflict with, the other (Alonso *et al*. 1980: 377–439). CoRett, too, occasionally meddled unnecessarily, as when it declared that were it to be in charge of regularization in the settlement of Ajusco, the cost to residents would be much lower than that proposed by FIDEURBE (López Díaz 1978). Coming precisely at a time when the latter agency was trying to secure the co-operation of *colonos* it is difficult to interpret CoRett's action as anything but deliberate sabotage.

Furthermore, conflict between agencies was facilitated by the structure of patron–client links which agency directors and personnel were expected to form with individual communities and by the proliferation of different leadership groups within each settlement, particularly the most conflictive. Each group of residents led, invariably, to a different agency so that it was common for one group to elicit support from the *procurador*; another would seek out the head of FIDEURBE while others would go to the local *delegado* (Alonso *et al*. 1980). At the same time, when a group felt really threatened they approached the president himself, who appeared well disposed to receiving their delegations and to listening to their case. As a result rumour abounded, contradictory policies were espoused, and orders were countermanded. One agency head bemoaned the frequent practice of calling agency heads to open hearings with the president which had the effect of undermining their authority without reducing their responsibility. Another described the experience as like being on a 'constant war footing'.

Whether this bureaucratic structure and functioning was the result of accident or design is a matter for speculation. However, the important point to recognize is its *functionality* for the Echeverría administration. The existence of several agencies, all apparently active on behalf of the poor, gave the impression that much was being done. Important also was the personal contact that Echeverría maintained with grassroots organizations and which he demanded also from his agency directors. The president could appear as arbitrator on behalf of selected groups (Connolly 1982). Also, where one agency threatened to become too powerful, or another too weak, he could shift his support to re-establish the balance.[5] Both land and the bureaucracy itself became the cannon fodder for political mediation by Echeverría.

A third way in which political mediation was achieved throughout this period was the identification of land regularization as an *issue* in its own right. Significantly, in no other country does regularization feature with such prominence (Gilbert & Ward 1985). But in Mexico regularization emerged as having critical importance from 1971 onwards. It was not new: various settlements had been legalized through expropriation since the late 1930s

(Varley 1985). However, the creation of a battery of agencies to provide full legal title to *colonos* was an innovation. Moreover, it can be argued that it reflected governmental needs more than those of residents. The concern of *colonos* was for security of tenure. The interpretation that this required full legal title was one provided by government rather than by the residents themselves. Full tenure was not required before *colonos* could sell their plots, not was it necessary for services to be installed, for this demand had usually been waived since the early 1960s. Security of tenure could easily have been provided by simple recognition of *de facto* occupancy and did not require full legalization through expropriation, indemnification and the drawing-up of property deeds and so on.

At this time regularization was not viewed by government as a *means* to an end. It was not conceived as a mechanism to incorporate the populace into the tax base, nor as a first step to recoup systematically government investment in services and utilities. Neither was it viewed as a requirement for the exercise of greater control over planning and building activities. These considerations came later. Rather regularization under Echeverría was an *end in itself*. It became the key ingredient around which state–community mediation was channelled. The struggle for legal tenure became paramount compared with water provision, drainage or any other urban service. Regularization was the one issue most likely to involve residents in popular mobilization.[6] Moreover, when analysed comparatively with other cities, it appeared as a significant issue only in Mexico (Gilbert & Ward 1985).

A fourth aspect of political mediation during the period came through the PRI. Although the party's direct control over settlement affairs had suffered as a result of the creation of new agencies responsible for regularization and housing with whom it had little influence, the proliferation of factions and groups rife in each settlement at this time provided ample room in which the PRI could manoeuvre. Different leaders sought legitimacy through the creation of vertical clientelist links created with various 'patrons'. This 'splitting' or hiving-off of several factions within a single settlement was not seriously challenged until 1977. Until then it offered both advantages as well as disadvantages to the Executive. On the one hand it gave rise to intra-settlement conflict which often spilt over into violence and caused embarrassment. On the other hand, the fact that no one leader had absolute authority enhanced the potential for manipulation of different factions by both the PRI and the government. Within this overall structure the PRI sought to project itself as having influence in the securement of essential services and land tenure, and was able to mobilize quite successfully within the free-for-all of settlement bargaining of the day. In the State of Mexico the party's main task was to penetrate the mass-based MRC and its sister organization in the *Quinta Zona* of Ecatepec. By classic methods of co-option and infiltration, the CNOP successfully undermined the potency of these organizations by 1976 (Cisneros n.d.).

In terms of government intervention to stimulate the supply of land to low-income groups, this period was no more interventionist than preceding decades. Although the state began to control the excesses of company developers of irregular settlement no attempt was made to tackle the *ejidal* land development sector which was now the most important means of land acquisition for the poor. While efforts were established through INDECO and INFONAVIT to develop land reserves for future use, these were very limited in size and potential (Makin 1984: 348). CoRett had wide-ranging responsibilities for the regularization of irregular settlement on *ejidal* land and for the *development* of low-income subdivisions on suitably located *ejidos* (*Diario Oficial*, 7 August 1973). The latter function, if it had been seriously pursued, would have offered the state a major opportunity of developing land supply for the poor. However, strong opposition from the *ejidal* sector emasculated this area of potential responsibility and it was subsequently withdrawn from CoRett's charter (*Diario Oficial*, 3 April 1979). The Agrarian Sector preferred to view CoRett's brief as one of legalizing the illegal land sales perpetrated by *ejidatarios* and of compensating the latter for the loss of their lands as part of the regularization process. It is difficult to see how this system of double payment, first from the would-be *colono*, and, secondly, from the government to compensate for the 'loss' of land, could fail to stimulate further irregularity (Ward 1983, Varley 1985). Anything that interfered with the process which worked firmly to the advantage of some *ejidatarios* was to be resisted. Indeed, for the state, the process also had certain attractions: the *ejido* sector upon which it depended for considerable political support was mollified; at the same time the supply of low-cost land for the poor was sustained. While the principal agents of land development had changed, government passivity in the matter of land provision had not.

Several large-scale invasions of land such as at Santo Domingo and Padierna occurred during this period and were partly an indirect response to government policy. Presidential statements to the effect that the poor would be supported in their struggle for housing were interpreted as support for land captures.[7] The bureaucratic structure created to deal with irregularity and the way in which it functioned throughout this period fuelled the propensity for invasions. Another cause of invasions was as a last resort on lands where *ejidatarios* were blocking the aspirations of other would-be settlement leaders.

The changes that were initiated by the state during the period 1971–6 appear to have been a direct result of the crisis proportions that unserviced and unrecognized settlement had reached by 1970. The flashpoint was provided by the payments strike initiated by the MRC. The chemistry was, in many ways, provided by Echeverría himself. His concern to appear responsive to the poor, and his increasing need to be able to mobilize them on his behalf at public rallies, led to the creation of a number of agencies responsible for regularization. In responding to the problem of illegal land development, the Executive sought to turn the land issue to political advantage. As far as land provision for low-income groups was concerned, the government ducked the problem. Instead of penalizing company developers, it allowed them to withdraw from the low-income real estate arena with most of their profits intact. Neither did it confront the illegal supply of land by the *ejidal* sector. By allowing CoRett's functions to be carefully restricted to the regularization and compensation of *ejido* lands it actually encouraged further irregularity.

Post-1977 initiatives: the exercise of more efficient controls over illegal land development
Since the end of Echeverría's government, although the underlying aim of land policy has remained one of maintenance of social control, the methods to achieve this have altered quite significantly. Broadly, policies have sought to exercise greater control over the process of land provision for low-income groups, and to make regularization procedures more efficient.

For the first time the state has responded sharply to company-led, low-income subdivisions. Several settlements have been 'embargoed' by the State of Mexico government: an option always open to previous administrations yet not exercised. It is usually achieved by requiring land developers to comply with servicing norms, and to make immediate payments of massive amounts of backdated taxes and fines relating to improper management of the subdivision. Failure to comply results in the development being sequestrated by the State authorities. However, as we have observed, this initiative has come too late to affect land provision significantly. Rather it is a mechanism to expedite regularization of existing settlements by transferring them from private to public hands. Also, the relative strength of the company subdividers has waned as they have gradually withdrawn from the low-income market.

Invasions, too, are no longer tolerated. During 1977–9 firm action was undertaken by the Federal District authorities to remove occupiers of newly established settlements. In one large-scale invasion attempt in the south of the city named after the president's wife, *colonos* were evicted each time they reoccupied the land. Their temporary houses were destroyed despite injunctions taken out against the authorities to prevent this from happening. Eventually they gave up and the land remained vacant. Explicit instructions were given by the mayor to *delegados* to resist all new occupation attempts and to raise the surveillance of vacant land. As we observed in the previous chapter, the existence of a Federal District Plan which attempts to define existing and future land uses may be used to justify the decision to eradicate a newly established settlement.

The combined 'clamp-down' on subdivisions and on invasions has meant that the only source of land for the poor is within the *ejidal* sector. Yet little attempt has been made by successive governments to restrict illegal sales by *ejidatarios*. In 1979 an Inter-Sector Commission was established, comprising the Ministries of Agrarian Reform and Human Settlements and CoRett, in an attempt to expedite the identification and expropriation of *ejidos* whose land would be affected by future urban growth. Although this might offer a major step forward in the acquisition of rural land for long-term urban development, in the absence of additional preventive measures it is unlikely to succeed in controlling land alienation by *ejidatarios* in the short or medium term. Quite the opposite: faced with the danger of government intervention to deny them the possibility of illegally selling land, it is likely to stimulate them to sell or to find ways of slowing up the process of handover to government.

Recent initiatives suggest that government may be ready to impose constraints upon the illegal sale of *ejidal* land. Miguel De la Madrid, in his manifesto circulated during his presidential campaign, explicitly referred to the unscrupulous speculation on *ejidal* plots and identified a need to establish policies that would stimulate the creation of land reserves (De la Madrid 1982: vol. 5, 243–4). However, whether or not the administration will take a strong stand against the abuse of *ejidal* land sales remains to be seen. Certainly SEDUE have been actively expropriating *ejidal* land throughout the country to create land reserves for long-term urban development. Also, given that the proportion of the total number of *ejidatarios* involved in these so-called *ejidos de oro* is relatively small, it should be quite an easy matter for the government, if it wished, to drive a wedge between the minority and the majority. But there are other strong vested interests to consider, particularly within the Agrarian Reform Ministry (Varley 1985). Although firm action against particular *ejidatarios* might represent a responsible undertaking in technical terms, politically it might be seen to be irresponsible because it would create conflict with those vested interests. By reducing the supply of land to low-income groups it would also engender potential conflict with the poor: from the government's point of view, better to leave well alone. Therefore it seems unlikely in the short term that the government will intervene determinedly against illegal developments on *ejidal* land, though it may seek to impose some constraints upon their present freedom of activity.

The regularization of land in existing settlements has intensified since 1977. Agencies responsible for regularization have become more efficient, and the number of titles issued each year has risen considerably in part as a response to efforts to simplify the process. But regularization has also undergone an important qualitative change. Since 1977 it has become both a means to an end as well as an end in its own right. When interviewing residents it became apparent that regularization is linked to taxation policies and, in particular, to attempts to raise the tax base of the city. Registration of dwellings rose sharply after 1978 and was considerably higher during the López Portillo administration than under the preceding government. Although the proportion of ordinary income of the Federal District provided by the rates has declined considerably over the period 1969–79, this reflects the growing importance of alternative sources of taxation relative to rates (*predial*). In real terms the annual yield from the rates has been maintained (Makin 1984: 313a). At the individual household level this policy is clearly observed: either when drawing up titles for inscription in the property register, or soon afterwards, the authorities attempt to 'clear' outstanding land tax debts that the *colono* is deemed to have. These may comprise rates chargeable retrospectively for up to a maximum of five years.

However, they often also include a range of other charges. In different settlements I found multiple examples of valorization taxes relating to motorway developments undertaken several years earlier; charges for construction permissions and apparently arbitrary fines. Often failure to pay meant that surcharges were also added. Where residents protested either through their leaders or *en masse*, then the amounts charged became negotiable and, more often than not, a discount was arranged. This demonstrates how the authorities sought both to raise Treasury resources as well as to use the procedure as a dimension of political mediation and control. The existence of a deliberate policy link between regularization and taxation was freely admitted by officials in the cadastral office of the Federal District.

Once legal title is achieved residents are subject to periodic charges for rates. It also becomes much easier for the authorities to ensure payment for services that are subsequently installed; and charges are added to the bill sent by the tax office. Similarly, inscription in the Property Registry facilitates future land-use planning. Theoretically planning permission must be sought for building construction and improvements. Whether the poor will assiduously seek such permissions is another matter, but there is now the facility (not usually exercised) for the authorities to check whether authorization has been obtained and to penalize cases where it has not.

The structure of the land and urban development bureaucracy and the way in which it behaves changed substantially from 1977 onwards. This was partly a result of the overall streamlining of the various sectors of government activity initiated by López Portillo as part of his Administrative Reform. It was also indicative of the growing technocratization of the bureaucracy in which politicians have been replaced by professionals (*técnicos*). In the Federal District it was part of a conscious effort to change the nature of state–community relations and to make land regularization more efficient and less politicized.

The number of agencies with responsibilities for regularization were reduced (Fig. 4.2). Specifically, at the national level INDECO became primarily a housing agency with responsibility for the unsalaried population and no longer had functions of land regularization. The PCP and FIDEURBE were absorbed by a new Commission for Urban Development (CODEUR). Although this new agency had a wide range of duties, budgetary restrictions meant that in effect its primary task became one of regularization of property titles. CoRett, as we have seen, continued with clearly defined responsibilities for regularization of *ejidal* property which would not be duplicated by other agencies. In the State of Mexico FINEZA continued, but was now simply winding up the delivery of titles under its previous agreement. An important new agency for land regularization emerged. 'Plan Sagitario' was an agency without any legal status and was really what its name suggests – a programme of land regularization. On the orders of the State governor it was designed to bring together all the relevant parties of the State of Mexico bureaucracy into a single programme that would expedite the granting of land titles to plot holders. The regularization functions of AURIS and FINEZA, although nominally separate, were, in effect, subsumed within the programme. The important point is not simply that overlaps were reduced but that authority was invested in a specific agency and not shared between them as had happened before. Each got on with the job for which it was responsible and kept out of the other's way.

The process of streamlining and technocratization has continued since 1982. In the State of Mexico a new regularization agency has emerged (CRESEM) to replace its predecessors. In the Federal District CODEUR has disappeared but its regularization functions remain in an independent body which had emerged by the early 1980s (DART). Significantly, it forms part of the Property Registry Department which collaborates closely with the cadastral office.

Throughout the period, increased responsibility did not mean that budgets were much greater than before; by and large they remained low and barely enough to cover staffing costs. But they were more secure and less likely to fluctuate from year to year. Inadequate funding meant that among its various functions CODEUR could do little more than regularize land titles. In its 1978 submission for financing it made a case for the funds required to carry out all of its duties, but recognizing that this was a financial impossibility also put forward carefully scaled-down estimates of absolute priority items. The appropriation it eventually received was one-fifteenth of the sum requested. One attribute of regularization is that it is cheap and makes little demand on scarce resources.

The structure of negotiating land regularization has also changed (Ward 1981a). The proliferation of different competing leadership factions within a single settlement is largely a feature of the past. Government officials usually recognize only the elected neighbourhood president who forms part of the *junta de vecinos* structure, and negotiate only with that person. The free-for-all of competitive bargaining that was typical of Echeverría's administration, to-gether with the existence of overlapping agency responsibilities that encouraged it, have been replaced by a more closely structured arrangement. Residents' liaison is with a single institution. Often the linkage is a direct one between individual *colono* and the agency, and the influence of the local leader or intermediaries has been dissolved almost entirely (Varley 1985). During my fieldwork it became apparent that where bills were sent by the Treasury to residents for retrospective rates or taxes, these were usually delivered in batches to a random scatter of households throughout the settlement. The aim appeared to be one of minimizing the likelihood of collective action. Where residents mobilized to complain, they were usually directed through the *junta de vecinos* structure and the local *delegado*. Rarely was the mayor or president approached.

The emergence of this singular structure to replace the earlier 'free-for-all' system has not led to any major loss of control by the authorities, as I shall argue in the next chapter. However, it has led to an erosion of opportunities for the PRI to intervene in land regularization issues. The party and the DDF clashed in 1979 when the former tried to take responsibility for a large rally at which thousands of land titles were to be presented to low-income residents. Although ultimately they succeeded in achieving a high profile at the event, it was not without widespread criticism in the press and considerable embarrassment to top government officials. Of course, around election times the PRI, like most other political parties, can be found 'leading' delegations of *colonos* and their leaders to government offices in order to press the local neighbourhood's claims to regularization, or to denounce excess charges. But this is not exclusive to the PRI, nor is it usually effective in changing the agency's programme. Nor does it especially impress the leaders and *colonos* who have become quite realistic in their assessment of what the PRI can, and cannot, deliver.

Therefore, as the bureaucracy has established more 'technical' routines in handling regularization, so the PRI has had less opportunity to use land as a source of patronage. Also, of course, the declining absolute number of people still without legal title will have the same effect. But the fact that the PRI is still expected to 'deliver' the vote at elections, yet has lost some of its previous influence over the distribution of urban resources, is not likely to be missed by party militants and poses an interesting dilemma for both government and party alike. It is a dilemma which I propose to examine in greater detail in the following chapter.

Several important points emerge from this review of changing government response to irregular settlement. We have seen that land is an important mechanism for political mediation in Mexico City. So far as the provision of land is concerned the state's response has been passive. In choosing not to act against the real estate companies or against those responsible for *ejidal* land sales, it has favoured certain interests at the expense of the poor, and condoned illegal practices. At the same time the illegal supply of land for low-income groups has been maintained. However, there are signs that the state is contemplating more direct action against land developers. But past experience suggests that this is most likely to happen when serious social unrest threatens the state's ability to maintain social order. State intervention may become more likely once formerly powerful interest groups have shown that they are prepared to withdraw from an area of activity in which they were previously involved – as happened in the case of the company developers in the State of Mexico.

In establishing policy towards existing irregular settlement the covert aims of the state appear to have been paramount. The state has sought to use the land issue as a means of extending its influence over the poor and of maintaining their quiescence. The way in which this has been achieved has altered significantly in recent years. Prior to 1977 control was sought primarily by political manipulation, co-option and patron–client links with the poor. Since that date, while social stability and social passivity remain fundamental goals, the state has developed a more structured framework in which to achieve them. Increasingly, it depends for its legitimacy and support on greater efficiency and delivery of resources desired by *colonos*, and less upon traditional forms of mediation such as patron–clientelism and the PRI apparatus. In Mexico regularization has become an important element in the political calculus. The nature of regularization has evolved to reflect state priorities rather than those of low-income groups. It is not simply a means of extending full property titles to the poor, but is increasingly a means of incorporating them into the tax base.

Changing access to land for the poor

Analysis so far in this chapter has attempted to explain the rationale for state and bureaucracy response towards irregular settlements. We have observed that this response has become more interventionist since the late 1960s. There appear to be much tighter controls upon land invasions, and large-scale subdivisions by private landowners are no longer condoned. Only on *ejidal* land is state response equivocal, and, in the 1980s, this provides the primary opportunity for low-income households to break into the land market.

These changes suggest that access to land ought to have become more difficult in recent years and the temptation is to accept this hypothesis without question. There is a growing body of literature for Third World cities which asserts that opportunities for the poor to gain a foothold in the land market are declining. Several studies suggest that earlier 'informal' processes of land supply have begun to break down with the result that land acquisition has become more difficult (Baross 1983). If this has happened then it ought to be testable. In capitalist economies one would associate growing scarcity with higher prices: the cost of land should be increasing in real terms if the proposition is to be sustained. Similarly, proportionately less people will enter the land market as 'owners' and far more will be forced to opt for rental accommodation or to share with kinsmen. As a concomitant, if purchase of land is more expensive, and the savings required are much greater than before, then one would expect the average age of household heads at the time of lot acquisition to have risen as they are forced to remain in non-ownership for a longer period than earlier cohorts (Gilbert 1983: 466). Densities, too, should have risen, not simply in established, 'consolidating' self-build settlements but, more specifically, in newly formed irregular settlements. As a result of price increases and greater demand, one would expect average plot sizes to diminish. The following analysis takes each of these points in turn and begins by examining the most contentious element: that of land price trends.

Trends in the costs of land acquisition
Using our PIHLU data as well as those of other studies, I have examined whether the acquisition cost of land in Mexico City and in other Latin American cities has changed in any consistent way. Accurate data are difficult to gather. Most studies are not comprehensive of the city as a whole but relate to certain types of land development. Usually these are middle-income residential areas which vary enormously in terms of prestige, location, levels of service

provision, and income group. Comparability between data collected in different settlements is, therefore, extremely difficult. There are even fewer studies of land prices in low-income settlements and here, too, one confronts the problem of comparing irregular settlements (*barrios*) that are not strictly speaking alike. Mode of land acquisition (invasion versus subdivision), the speed of initial occupancy, the location, the mix of low-income households and other better-off groups, all work against meaningful comparison. The collection of data within each settlement also presents problems. Not all plots have equal market value at a given time; those further away from principal thoroughfares or higher up a hillside may not fetch such high prices as other plots that are more conveniently situated. Similarly, corner plots or those strategically located for business activities will usually demand a higher asking price. Add to this the technical difficulties of collecting data through interviews, where some respondents are unwilling to disclose that they made illegal payments for the land, or fail to describe fully payments to a variety of agents (original landowner, government for regularization, etc.) and the problem becomes even more complicated. Clearly this is land on which a statistical purist would be reluctant to tread.

Nevertheless it is important to make comparisons, but when doing so we must always bear in mind the limitations and possible distortions introduced through the nature of the data. In the PIHLU study we attempted to maximize comparability by selecting settlements that were at an equivalent stage of urbanization. Moreover, in the data analysis I have been careful to screen out later arrivals who did not acquire land in the early phase of settlement consolidation. Thus *traspasos* between consecutive plot owners were excluded. I have also attempted, where possible, to check our data against other sources. Finally, my concern was not one of a statistical purist. I wanted to know whether or not broad trends in land prices and tenure structure were discernible and, if so, in which direction these trends might point our understanding about the relative ease of land acquisition in Mexico.

The argument that land prices are increasing is a compelling one which, as Gilbert and Gugler point out (1982: 91–2), many urban analysts often accept without thorough investigation. For example, Evers (1977: 782), when writing about Asian cities, noted that 'population increase and other social processes have intensified the pressure on urban land and have led, in the 1970s, to a wave of land speculation and spiralling land prices'. In São Paulo land prices appear to have increased dramatically between 1968 and 1974 (Haddad 1982). It is certainly true that nominal land prices have risen in Latin American cities, but whether this also represents an increase in real terms, allowing for inflation, is not always made clear (Unikel 1972, Legorreta 1983).

In Mexico City analyses of land price trends are almost non-existent. One notable exception is Makin's (1984) study of advertised sale prices of plots in six middle-income zones. While recognizing that these are 'asking-prices' and are not actual prices charged, he argues, correctly, that the bias was likely to be built in throughout the period and should not, therefore, affect the overall trend. Four of the six neighbourhoods yielded data suitable for statistical analysis, and in these areas Makin found that prices increased by between 2.6% and 6.5% per annum over a 30-year period. In the neighbourhood of Del Valle, for which the record was most complete, the increase was 4.3% per annum over the whole period, and 2.8% annually between 1970 and 1981. Overall the data suggest that prices have increased substantially in recent decades and continued to rise during the 1970s. Makin (1984: 296) concludes that it is 'probable that prices have been increasing above mean household incomes and is hence likely that an increasing proportion of households are barred from formal land markets'. In response many middle income and lower-middle income households have entered the apartment and condominium market instead.

But what about land prices in irregular settlements? Bearing in mind the caveats to which I referred earlier relating to the collection of these data, the analysis reveals that real land prices have barely increased between 1968 and 1978 (Table 4.1). Price fluctuations that appear on Table 4.1 are most marked in the socially mixed-income *ejido* settlements of Padierna and San Jerónimo (column 3) in the south-west of the city, but this reflects the small sample size for individual years in which rich households had purchased land (1970 and 1972) compared with years when the sample comprised residents who were un-equivocally poor (for example, 1971, columns 1 and 2). Broadly, though, prices in subdivisions appear to have increased by about one-half over the ten years, while the cost of purchase into *ejidal* land has crept up by perhaps about one-third. The costs of acquiring plots through 'invasion' (see note b on Table 4.1) have remained approximately stable.

When collecting these data it became apparent that in the case of land acquisition on *ejidos* the price charged was often a matter for negotiation between vendor or leader and would-be settler. *Ejidatarios* would often try to judge how much they could extract from an applicant. Hence prospective buyers who were better off, or who wanted larger than normal plots, were invariably charged more. Alternatively, those who were clearly low-income, or who were friends of the vendor or were recommended to him, would pay much less. Charges appeared to be more standardized and less arbitrary in illegal subdivisions and where the sale of *ejidal* land was being promoted by the *comisariado* rather than an individual *ejidatario*.[8]

Therefore, the data do not suggest enormous increases in real land prices, at least not up until the late 1970s when my survey ended. This does not mean that ease of access has remained the same throughout, though one would expect an increase in land costs as land becomes more scarce. The fact that prices have not increased greatly may be a function of the settlements selected, or that land prices were over-inflated during the late 1960s when subdivisions were at their height, and are relatively underpriced in subsequent *ejidal* land sales. Moreover, conditions may have changed since 1979. Similar work in Querétaro using an identical methodology shows that *ejidal* land sales doubled in price in real terms

Table 4.1 Price trends for land acquisition in different types of low-income settlement, in constant (1978) pesos per square metre.

	Ejidos[a]					Mean plot size (square metres)[d]
	Low income		Mixed		'Sub-	
Year acquired	(1)	(2)	(3)	'Invasions'[b]	divisions'[c]	
1968	62	95	258	74	89	296
1969	101	42	106	65	64	296
1970	42	71	664	67	107	237
1971	43	42	57	62	96	240
1972	128	72	564	64	118	261
1973	36	53	—	44	109	227
1974	90	218	313	98	186	220
1975	—	63	—	61	115	211
1976	71	152	—	65	145	172
1977	—	75	—	56	144	162
1978	60	—	560	47	96	199
total no. of cases	40	48	23	114	145	330

Sources and notes

[a] Data in column 1 are provided by Ann Varley and relate to two low-income settlements in the north of the city (San Jóse de Los Leones II, and Loma de la Palma). Data in column 2 are also unequivocally for a low-income settlement located in the north, that of Chalma Guadalupe, and are derived from the PIHLU study. Column 3 data are presented separately because they relate to San Jerónimo and Padierna in the south-west where many purchasers were middle-income and were charged much higher prices.

[b] Here were included those who unequivocally squatted on the land together with people who received a plot free from leaders. Prices in this column relate mostly to charges for regularization and are not, strictly, comparable with the other data which relate to acquisition. They are also somewhat inflated because charges for regularization usually come a considerable time after the moment of acquisition. Calculations for constant prices were pegged to year of arrival and therefore will exaggerate the actual real cost of regularization. They are included in the table to provide an approximate reference point to other means of land acquisition. Source is the PIHLU study.

[c] Subdivisions include all those who bought from a subdivider, be it a company, an *ejidatario* or *comisariado ejidal*, or the cooperatively organized land purchase and subdivision in Liberales. Cases disaggregated at column 2 are also included here. Source is the PIHLU study.

[d] Average plot size data are for all owners, PIHLU survey (1979).

between 1970 and 1983, with an especially marked increase since 1979 during which time no new settlements were formed (Chant 1984: 119).

So far I have considered price trends for land acquisition in newly formed irregular settlements. It is important to recognize that, once established, land prices in irregular settlement may increase dramatically in real terms and represent a considerable asset for the pioneer household (Moser 1982). Makin (1984) examined cadastral land values between 1962 and 1974 for four Mexico City low-income settlements in Ixtapalapa and Ixtacalco, and found an average annual increase of 11%. This was much higher than the increase recorded for middle-income residential districts using sales prices. In Sector Popular, a low-income settlement created in 1952, the real land value more than tripled between 1962 and 1974. Even adjusting for real salary increases during the period, anyone wanting to buy land in Sector Popular in the 1970s would receive far less for their money than ten years earlier. In Mexico land prices have a lower initial base rate due to the greater tenure insecurity and complete absence of services. However, once *de facto* tenure is assured then prices increase. Improvements to the settlement, house consolidation, and the arrival of services and regularization all accelerate this process. Nevertheless this is only good news to the original occupiers: later arrivals must pay a much higher price for land and, inevitably, this will exclude most of the poor. Makin (1984: 301), referring to *colonos*, concludes that 'paradoxically their exclusion from regular entry into formal land markets may result in their obtaining an asset which is likely to appreciate at a much faster rate than mean rates of land value increase in the formal market'.

The affordability of land purchase in Mexico City

Changing land prices provide an indication about whether access is becoming more or less difficult over time, but it is necessary to ask, also, whether the poor can afford to buy land. Although most low-income households may be willing to spend up to about one-third of their wages on accommodation, it is important to recognize that land purchase is only one of the many costs involved in successful consolidation – a point to which I shall return in Chapter 5. In order to examine the relative cost of land the PIHLU data were analysed in two ways: first, the unit cost of land; second, unit cost as a proportion of wages (Gilbert & Ward 1985). Moreover, the accuracy of our data was checked against that of other studies and, generally, our findings proved very similar.[9] For subdivisions there were large discrepancies between my data and others', suggesting that I had under-reported the costs of acquisition from company developers. The difference is in part a result of the settlements selected in the PIHLU study where land prices certainly appear to be cheaper than in many other subdivisions, but it also reflects the fact that other studies have sought to demonstrate the expense of land acquisition and may have selected settlements to reflect this. However, it seems likely that my data under-report somewhat the costs of subdivision, making land acquisition appear easier than it actually was.

Compared with data gathered for Bogotá, the price of land acquisition in Mexico appears to be much lower. In Mexico City the price paid in constant (1978) US dollars per square metre was $4.98 for those who bought into a subdivision and $2.91 for those who invaded (Gilbert & Ward 1985: 111). This compares with $8.2 in Bogotá for those who purchased land. Expressed another way, we calculated the area that could be acquired in each city for the minimum salary and for the average monthly salary of low-income residents. These data indicate that costs are substantially higher in Bogotá than Mexico. It also suggests that the cost of land acquisition has been at a price that has been affordable to low-income households in Mexico City. However, there is some validity in the argument that given the poor location of these lands, their unsuitability to urbanization and their lack of services and utilities, the prices paid were excessive compared with the unit cost of land in properly developed middle-income subdivisions (Connolly 1982, Sudra 1976).

Careful interpretation of these findings is required. They do not mean that land acquisition in Mexico is easy. In many ways it is more difficult than in Bogotá as there are enormous social costs involved in living in a state of high insecurity without services for months and even years on end. As we have observed it is this feature of land acquisition in Mexico that makes the process relatively cheap. Unlike their Mexican counterparts, self-builders in Bogotá have security of tenure from the moment that they buy their parcel of land. As a result they do not have to occupy their plot from the outset but can carry on living elsewhere while they begin to build a new home on their new plot. There is an average lapse of 1.2 years between acquisition and moving in in Bogotá, and some 45% of owners had not occupied their lot for at least a full year after they had bought it. In contrast in Mexico City three-quarters of all owners moved on to their plot as soon as they acquired it. In Mexico, whether an individual buys or invades makes no difference: the plot must be occupied from the outset otherwise someone else may move in. Only after tenurial assurances are met do prices rise in Mexico City, and there seems little doubt that the early purchase price differential with Bogotá is quickly eroded. Nevertheless, it is a fact that for those who were prepared to suffer, land has been quite freely available to the poor at prices they could afford.

The effects of changing acquisition costs

If costs have increased in real terms, or if access is becoming more difficult now that tighter controls are being exercised over new attempts to invade or to subdivide land, then this ought to be reflected by other indicators and by responses that the poor make in their efforts to find suitable shelter.

Changing plot size might be expected to reflect rising prices. Indeed, comparison of average plot sizes in Mexico City (234 square metres), Bogotá (137 square metres) and Valencia in Venezuela (452 square metres), where land is very cheap, suggests that *prima facie* there is a direct relationship between the cost of land acquisition and the size of plot purchased. Therefore, if land costs have increased in recent years, or if access has become more difficult, then we might expect average plot sizes to have declined. This appears to be borne out by the data in Table 4.1 for the period 1968–78. Moreover, if we exclude those who invaded, the decline in plot size registered by those who have bought land in recent years is even more marked. Whereas some 44% of those who purchased prior to 1970 bought a plot of more than 250 square metres in area, only 11% bought a similar sized plot after that date.

Tenure, too, might be expected to reflect growing difficulty of land acquisition. Urbanization generally leads to higher rates of renting, but in

Mexico City the proportion of owners has risen substantially from 1960 onwards, largely reflecting the expansion of the population in irregular settlements.[10] Since 1970, although the *colonias* have continued to grow, much of the increase is due to densification within existing settlements, especially the growth of rental opportunities (Brown 1972, COPEVI 1978). Specifically, a greater proportion of the population will find that their entry into the land market is delayed or even closed permanently. For example, the average age of owners when they secured their plot was 33.6 years. Renters' average age at the time of survey was already 33.4 years, suggesting that recent and future cohorts of renters will be significantly older if and when they enter the land market as owners. Indeed, almost half of the renters included in the sample survey were older than the average age at which their owner counterparts had moved to their plots.

Alternatively, sharing plots with kin is an important feature of tenure arrangements in *colonias populares* in Mexico (comprising 14% of all households in the survey settlements). Recent migrants may be fortunate enough to be allowed to set up their own homes independently in the plot of a kinsman. More usually, sharing evolves where children get married and want to live apart from parents and in-laws (Ward 1976b). For them, sharing may be a temporary measure while they save cash that would otherwise have been spent on rent; or it may be permanent where the parents expect the child to inherit the plot or a part of it.

Renting is also important and rises with settlement age and increasing cadastral land values (comprising 10% of households in the survey settlements). Usually renting is organized on a small-scale basis. Landlords are often *colonos* who let a part of their own plot or, where they acquired more than one lot during the formation of the settlement, then the additional ones may be subdivided into rental tenements. These usually comprise a series of single brick-built rooms around a narrow patio in which the shared toilets and washing facilities are located. Occasionally landlords are outsiders who buy out pioneer residents and who may have a number of different plots. However, large-scale or corporate landlordism is not yet a feature of *colonias populares* in Mexico, nor does it appear to be significant elsewhere in Latin America (Geisse & Sabatini 1982, Gilbert 1983).

Conclusion

Since the Revolution land redistribution and agrarian reform have offered a primary medium for political mediation in Mexico. Although the pace of redistribution has varied with different presidents, none has dared to abandon or to ignore the *campesino* sector (Hansen 1974, Varley 1985). We have observed in this chapter how the distribution of urban land and allocation of property titles have entered the mainstream of political mediation. By and large state response towards land provision has been passive, allowing private landlords, real-estate companies and a relatively small number of *ejidatarios* to alienate land for low-income groups. Where state intervention has occurred it is usually to advance those interests. Action against them is likely only when social unrest threatens to get out of hand, or once they have acknowledged a willingness to withdraw gracefully from illegal land sales. The counterpoint to this passivity is the state's increased willingness to intervene in regularizing property titles. Although this process is not new, it is only since 1970 that it has been developed for political advantage. Moreover, the nature of regularization has been carefully shaped to meet governmental needs. Specifically this entails the identification of full property title as both desirable and the only guarantee of ownership. The finer points of detail, the costs of regularization, and the speed with which it is carried out are all negotiable.

While land has emerged as a major urban issue over the last three *sexenios*, the way in which it has been managed alters with different administrations. In this respect the structure and functioning of the bureaucracy is all important. Under Echeverría the bureaucracy was carefully manipulated to encourage the opportunities for patron–clientelism and the paternalistic intervention of the president himself. This gave the appearance of activity on behalf of the poor and provided a medium for controlled mobilization of the poor for political purposes. Subsequent administrations have attempted to improve bureaucracy effectiveness as a principal means to achieve social stability and legitimacy. They are equally concerned to maintain social order, but the method and channels used are streamlined, more technocratic and consistent.

Although the poor have benefited, they have done so less than other social groups and at a cost of great hardship. At least some of this hardship could have been reduced had the state taken a more active line and provided land more cheaply than illegal developers, or ensured that it was provided in a more ordered and less exploitative way. The poor have not benefited equally, either. Low-income groups who have recently bought land or who are seeking to buy must pay a higher price in real terms than their predecessors. Also, for many contemporary renters the prospects are grim. Rising land costs and the lack of cheap land in suitable locations means that many will be obliged to rent accommodation over a longer period of their lives, and perhaps permanently.

Ideologically, too, the way in which the land issue has been managed has important ramifications. It encourages conservatism in so far as it extends property ownership to a greater proportion of the population. More import-antly, it encourages passivity and acquiescence through the nature of the relationship that is established between the poor and the state. Whether this comprises patron–clientelism, individual *colono*–bureaucracy links, or formally established channels of communication, the poor remain beholden to govern-ment for the supply of scarce resources. Negotiation is orientated towards issues of deciding how much regularization should cost, which settlements should be given priority, whether or not discounts are merited, and so on, and away from wider issues about the supply of land, the type of tenure security that is desired by residents, whether or not they should be paying rates at all given the absence of many basic services, whether or not they should be compensated for valorizing the land through communal efforts, and so on. Quiescence is further maintained by the existence of different ideological perspectives of owners and renters. However, the emergence of renters as a large minority group within many irregular settlements, and the fact that they are less likely to tolerate poor services and rising costs brought about by recent fiscal adjustments associated with regularization, suggests that they might provide a future caucus of more radical demand making. So far the state has ignored their specific position and needs. While great care has been taken to 'routinize' the demand making of low-income home owners, there has been an implicit assumption that non-owners in the *colonias populares* are numerically insignificant. This is no longer true, and the state has not yet devised a 'handle' on the manipulation of this particular group.

Notes

1 Elsewhere (Gilbert & Ward 1985) we have attempted to draw up a system of classification for irregular settlement in a variety of countries. See also Burgess (1985).

2 The history of land transfers before they came to be in the hands of the developers is interesting. Briefly, it was originally federal land which was privatized during the 1920s at low cost on the understanding that it would be improved for agricultural purposes (*bonificación*). These improvements were not undertaken and the government sought the restitution of the lands under its ownership. This led to litigation and the Supreme Court found against the government (Guerrero *et al.* 1974). Thereafter, during the 1940s, the land began to change hands and prices rose.

3 A good example of the involvement of the Oficina de Colonias in settlement affairs occurred in one of the survey settlements – Isidro Fabela. The CNOP and Agency staff were constantly engaged in overseeing leadership 'elections', and arranging the visit of Echeverría when he was presidential candidate. It was they who delivered pots of paint, trees and shrubs and so on with which to decorate the *colonia* prior to the Olympic Games. (The settlement lies alongside the southern ring motorway and is very near the Olympic Village.)

4 As we observed in Chapter 3 this breaks all the 'rules' within Mexican politics. Movement is from the bottom upwards through the various levels of the hierarchy and only rarely will someone 'jump' a level and go over the head of one's immediate boss (Smith 1979). To step sideways and form links with equivalent levels of the hierarchy in other institutions is a very serious matter and is indicative of a shift or a withdrawal of loyalty on the part of the individual or group concerned. It rarely happens and the formation of an urban social movement (MRC) indicated that the traditional form of government and PRI-organized mediation of 'divide and rule' had broken down.

5 AURIS suffered in a slightly different way, which sheds light on the way in which the bureaucracy itself is used for political purposes. Hank González's success as governor of the State of Mexico threatened to 'outshine' the president, such that Echeverría sought to clip his wings. Although most areas of activity found themselves cut back somewhat in 1974–5, AURIS in particular suffered as it was, in the words of its director, seen as the 'illegitimate son of Hank González'.

6 One section of the household survey in the PIHLU study sought information about the participation of household members in *barrio* meetings, petitioning, attendance at rallies, visits to government offices and to politicians and so on. The results of the survey showed, first, that participation measured in this way was higher in Mexico than in either Colombia or Venezuela but rarely involved a majority of residents (Table 5.2); and secondly, that in Mexico the issue most likely to mobilize residents was regularization of land tenure (Gilbert & Ward 1985).

7 In Santo Domingo several residents said that the president had stated in his first State of the Nation Address (*Informe*) that unused land would be made available to the poor for low-cost housing. I could find no reference to any such statement nor to any other that could be similarly construed. It is likely, therefore, that this was 'heard' secondhand from one of the leaders at a *colonia* meeting.

8 Similar findings have been reported by Varley (1985) and by Chant (1984) in their fieldwork in Mexico City and Querétaro respectively.

9 Costs of land in 1978 US dollars per square metre according to various studies are shown in Table 4.2.

Table 4.2 Different estimates for land costs in irregular settlements of Mexico City.

	Subdivisions	Invasions	Range
Our data	4.98	—	3·9– 8.3
		2.91	2.6– 4.6
FIDEURBE: Ajusco		3.5	—
FIDEURBE: Padierna		7.6	4.6– 7.6
Sudra (1976: 196)	5.4	—	—
Sudra (1976: 352)	22.0	—	—
Guerrero *et al.* (1974: 25)	19.9	—	—
Martín de la Rosa (1974)	23.2	—	15.5–31.0
Ward (1976b: 85)	23.0	—	—
Schteingart (1981: 20)	13.2	—	11.0–17.6

10 In Mexico City the census in 1970 only differentiated between 'owners' and 'non-owners'. According to the National Census the proportion of owners in 1960 was 19.8%, which increased to 41.6% in 1970 and to 52.7% by 1980. The rise between 1960 and 1970, although expected, is of such magnitude to suggest that the data are not strictly comparable. It is possible that owners without legal tenure were not included in the 1960 totals. However, the levelling off in the proportion of owners between 1970 and 1980 is indicative of the densification process to which I refer in the text.

5 The politics and costs of service provision

Once land has been acquired the poor turn their attention towards the introduction of urban services such as water, electricity, public transport, paved roads, street lighting, and of other public utilities including schools, covered markets, and health centres. Unlike most middle-income subdivisions where most of these services are installed from the outset, in irregular settlements they are usually provided only when the area is fully settled, and there may be long delays before an adequate service is obtained – if at all.

The factors which affect the introduction of basic services are complex. First, the nature of the service is important. Some services are given higher priority by residents than others: in Mexico City, for example, water and electricity usually rank as more important than paved roads, a market place or a health centre. Certain services such as water and drainage are 'lumpier' than others, in that they require larger investment and extensive preliminary public works to provide the primary and secondary networks, before development of a household network can be tackled. Inevitably this makes them more expensive and less easy to obtain.

A second factor that determines servicing levels relates to the nature of government and the servicing bureaucracy. Certain services are accorded higher priority by governments but the residents may not always concur with their ranking. Some agencies and departments are highly efficient while others are grossly inefficient. As we shall observe shortly, some departments within the bureaucracy follow strict technical criteria and procedures in determining who gets what, and how quickly. In these cases the incidence of queue jumping is reduced. Elsewhere, alternative criteria such as political contacts and well-placed bribes are important, with the result that the allocation of resources appears more arbitrary.

Thirdly, the characteristics of the individual community and its population are significant. Obviously location with respect to accessibility to existing services is important, as is the nature of the terrain and the ease with which any given service can be installed. Each of these factors will affect the likelihood of a service being provided and the speed of its introduction. But more important, perhaps, is the response of the residents. Those neighbourhoods that hustle, create a nuisance and embarrass the government may be more (or less) likely to get services than those that do not. Settlements which are politically aligned with the government or which enjoy particularly good contacts with key decision makers and politicians may be more successful than those that are less well connected. Some community leaders will work hard and honestly on behalf of the community, others are opportunistic and corrupt and may retard service provision. Widespread resident collaboration in public works may also be a necessary ingredient before a service is provided.

My concern in this chapter is to identify the impact of changing government commitment to provide urban services for the poor in Mexico City since the late 1960s. Specifically, in relation to the broad factors identified above, what are the crucial determinants of servicing policy and how have these changed over different administrations? Does the provision of public services, like access to land discussed in the preceding chapter, form part of the process of political mediation in Mexico?

First, I wish to examine the arguments about the growth of government intervention in Latin American cities and ask whether or not certain services are more readily provided by governments than by other organizations, and for what reasons. Secondly, I analyse recent efforts to improve the availability of domestic water and electricity supplies to irregular settlements and examine the procedures applied by the water and electricity supply agencies in deciding their servicing priorities. Thirdly, I evaluate the importance of community mobilization in determining service allocation. Different structures have emerged to channel state–community relations, but it is necessary to identify the relevance and purpose of these arrangements. In short, whose interest do they serve: the community or the state? Finally, have costs incurred by poor families in securing provision changed significantly in recent years? Can low-income residents afford the provision of services?

The growth of state intervention

An important question to emerge in recent years about public intervention is why the state takes responsibility for providing certain services and not others. For example, in an earlier study of housing and servicing in Mexico City, Bogotá and Valencia, we found that the private sector was more likely to be involved in activities such as the provision of transport, building materials and land development. On the other hand, the public sector invariably had sole responsibility for providing services such as water, drainage, main roads, and electricity. For some services, such as health care, education, and housing, responsibility was shared (Gilbert & Ward 1985). Sometimes public responsibility for servicing has been achieved by the state taking over private enterprise. In Mexico, for example, both the telephone and electricity services were, until relatively recently, run by private companies. A similar process may be observed in many industrialized countries, as in the United Kingdom where railways, telephones and many other essential services were nationalized many years ago. It will be interesting to observe whether recent attempts to reverse this process in the UK through privatization will find similar favour and application in Latin American countries.

Several writers have attempted to explain the growth of state intervention (O'Connor 1973, O'Donnel 1973, Collier 1979). In particular, Castells' work (1977, 1979) has attracted attention. In the case of advanced capitalist societies he argues that growing state intervention is an inevitable outcome of the falling rate of profit in the capitalist economy. In order to maintain the rate of capital accumulation the state undertakes responsibility for providing services that are 'collectively consumed'. Generally speaking these services are those which offer low profit to the private sector but for which there is rising demand from organized working classes: 'the intervention of the state becomes necessary in order to take charge of the sectors and services which are less profitable (from the point of view of capital) but necessary for the functioning of economic activity and/or appeasement of social conflicts' (Castells 1979: 18). State intervention is both direct and indirect but is concentrated in urban areas in the fields of infrastructure and servicing.

There are several problems with this argument, not least, perhaps, the recent moves towards privatization noted above. Also the term 'collective consumption' is an awkward one. It has been argued that many services simultaneously fulfil social consumption functions as well as stimulating economic growth which, clearly, relates to production (Lojkine 1976). Moreover, the collective element in social services is dubious in the sense that most collective services, such as health, public housing and education, are consumed individually (Pahl 1975, Harloe 1977, Saunders 1980). Also, while there has been a clear trend towards increasing responsibility by government for working classes, intervention has often grown fastest and been most concerted in areas linked to production, such as water, electricity, and transport infrastructure.

Furthermore, public intervention does not necessarily mean public ownership. The private sector may be heavily subsidized rather than being nationalized. In Mexico City until 1981, bus services were exclusively run by private companies with large state subsidies on fuel prices, a structure which continues to apply outside the Federal District. The state only tends to become the sole provider of a service when the size, complexity and inherently monopolistic nature of the product has created problems. Thus the private electricity company was incorporated into the public sector during the 1960s as demand for power increased.

Whether or not one accepts Castells' argument, certain services and activities appear more likely to fall under the wing of the state, and some will be accorded higher priority than others. The ranking will be for both growth and legitimacy reasons. Connolly (1981) argues that every activity falls along a continuum which runs from directly productive (and therefore beneficial to capital) to unproductive. A related continuum runs from activities with high social content (i.e., they both contain and integrate the population) to those with little social content. I would argue that in Mexico City concerted state intervention occurs primarily in those areas necessary to the acceleration of economic growth rather than in those vital to the welfare of the poor. When the poor benefit and receive water or electricity, it is after the needs of key productive enterprise and better-off social groups have been met. Social services such as education, housing, public health, and market facilities, which have little direct interest for the corporate sector, receive much lower priority and may even be neglected. The affluent can satisfy their needs through the private sector. Other groups are likely to benefit only in so far as they are able to exercise influence over the state. Inevitably, therefore, labour that is well organized or which occupies strategic industries such as power, railways, petroleum and so on is most likely to have its particular social needs met; the remainder will be less fortunate. We shall return to this point in greater detail when we examine health provision in Chapter 6.

Responsibility for housing and servicing in Mexico City

In earlier work we constructed a matrix to provide an overview of the differential involvement of public and private sectors in a range of activities such as water provision, health care, housing, land, transport and rubbish collection (Gilbert & Ward 1985: 138–41).[1] That matrix depicted the main responsibilities of the private and public sectors with respect to low-income and higher-income populations, at a variety of levels (local, regional and national). Briefly, we found that the private sector dominates in those areas such as land provision, building materials production and supply, and housing (housing either through large- and small-scale construction companies, or through self-building). On the other hand, the state is the major supplier of public utilities. With the exception of itinerant water sellers and the provision of bottled drinking water, it is the public sector which is wholly responsible for water and drainage, though different institutions are involved in procurement and supply, as will become apparent shortly. Electricity is much the same. Rubbish collection, health and public transport are the responsibility of both sectors. Our conclusion was that

> the state has become most involved in those activities which the private sector is unable to supply itself owing to the nature of the collective good . . . In general, the public sector has intervened most effectively and decisively in those areas essential to economic growth and in those sectors where more affluent residential groups could finance the servicing – notably water, drainage, electricity, roads and telephone . . . If state intervention has come in areas integrally linked in to the process of economic growth, there has also been a concern for social legitimation and welfare. (Gilbert & Ward 1985: 171)

Bureaucracy performance: the case of electricity and water

Electricity provision
Industrialization during the 1940s and 1950s required, among other things, provision of an adequate and reliable power supply. For many years federal investment in the Electricity Generating Commission (CFE) was a priority area and, once industrial and commercial needs had been met, there was ample supply to meet domestic needs as well. As a result most households in Mexico City enjoy a private metered service (Table 5.1). Although Mexico City's population is privileged in this respect, and a much higher proportion of dwellings nationally lacked a formal supply even in 1980, most urban areas throughout the country appeared to be reasonably well serviced. Most places, and the country as a whole, experienced a significant absolute and relative improvement in the distribution of domestic supplies between 1970 and 1980.

By and large supply has managed to keep pace with rapid city growth, both in the Federal District and in the surrounding municipalities. Moreover, many of those households recorded to be without an electricity supply will in fact receive current through informal, illegal hook-ups. This practice is especially common in recently formed settlements where groups of residents collaborate to buy cable and splice into a nearby overhead supply.

The supply of electricity in Mexico is primarily a 'technical' matter and the bureaucracy falls firmly at the technical end of the spectrum described in Chapter 3. Although 'political' interference by politicians or by high-ranking government officials to support the claims of particular groups is not unknown, it is relatively rare. There are several reasons for this. First, the overriding importance of power for industrial production demands an efficient and reliable system of supply that will not be subject to frequent political disturbance. Thus most of the personnel engaged in the electricity generation and supply bureaucracy are permanent employees whose jobs are unaffected by *sexenio* changes. Secondly, the bureaucracy itself comprises a simple and monopolistic structure. Within the Central Valley area there is a single institution with responsibility for providing the electricity service (the Companía de Luz y Fuerza del Centro S.A.) which since 1963 has been a state enterprise. Elsewhere in the Republic responsibility falls to the Federal Electricity Commission (CFE). Responsibilities are clearly demarcated and there is little of the inter-agency in-fighting that typifies so many areas of the Mexican governmental bureaucracy. Thirdly, the agencies have traditionally enjoyed a large degree of autonomy and have built up powerful, well-organized union structures, and this strengthens their ability to withstand constant political interference. Fourthly, electricity is not a scarce nor a particularly expensive commodity, and most would-be users who can easily be incorporated into the network will find themselves brought on-line fairly swiftly. From the Electricity Company's point of view, this is especially desirable where residents have a pirated supply for which they do not pay, and which may cause considerable damage to local substations.

Table 5.1 Levels of ownership and service provision in the Metropolitan Area of Mexico City and other large cities, 1970 and 1980.

	Total number of homes (000s)		Per cent owner households[a]		Per cent homes without electricity		Per cent homes without interior water supply[b]		Per cent homes without drainage[c]	
	1970	1980	1970	1980	1970	1980	1970	1980	1970	1980
Total country	8286.4	12074.6	66	68	41	25	61	50	59	43
Mexico City[d]	1477.3	2528.2	42	54	9	3	40	31	25	14
Tijuana	63.2	96.8	52	52	17	11	54	43	33	34
Ciudad Juárez	39.3	115.8	51	58	18	10	49	37	33	27
Torreón[d]	70.2	108.7	55	67	21	16	39	22	37	28
Monterrey[d]	204.0	346.3	50	68	14	6	37	28	29	20
Durango	31.7	55.4	60	68	29	12	42	27	40	30
Culiacán	57.5	96.5	71	79	38	16	65	52	68	60
Acapulco	41.1	80.9	65	70	33	20	37	57	56	47
Guadalajara[d]	221.6	400.9	46	52	nd	7	28	18	16	9
San Luis Potosí[d]	41.4	77.0	57	64	18	13	32	22	23	22
Toluca	39.5	62.7	64	63	29	13	53	35	46	24
Veracruz[d]	46.9	79.6	44	52	9	6	39	36	24	20
Tampico	40.0	56.5	45	55	15	12	47	50	25	25
Coatz-Minat[d]	38.9	66.2	59	62	28	29	63	68	40	35
Oaxaca	21.6	29.9	nd	65	31	21	63	51	50	44
Mérida[d]	42.1	90.1	71	77	16	7	44	36	46	40

Notes
[a] The classification of tenure altered between 1970 and 1980. In 1970 a twofold classification was adopted: owners and non-owners (which included accommodation that was rented, loaned or acquired through work). In 1980 the census identifies owners and renters, 'others'. Because of the ambiguity on the census forms it is likely that some 'sharers' were included under the owner category.
[b] In 1980 more than 66% of households had access to a piped water supply outside the dwelling – either elsewhere in the building or in the same plot.
[c] In 1970 defined as a 'hygienic system' for removing *aquas negras* (waste waters). In 1980 it was defined as those without drainage pipes. (The latter would include connections to mains drainage, a septic tank, or occasionally, a hole in the ground.)
[d] The Metropolitan Area of *Mexico City* includes the Federal District, Ecatepec, Naucalpan, Netzahualcóyotl, Tlalnepantla in 1970 together with the following additional localities in 1980: Atizapan, Coacalco, Tultitlán, Cuatitlán Izcalli, La Paz, Texcoco. The minimum threshold for inclusion was a population of 100 000. *Torreón* (Coahuila) includes Gómez Palacio and Ciudad Lerdo, State of Durango. *Monterrey* includes San Nicholas, Guadalupe, Garcia Garcia, and Catarina. *Guadalajara* includes Tlaquepaque, Zapopan and Tonalá. *San Luis Potosí* includes Soledad. *Veracruz* in 1980 includes Boca del Rio. *Coatz-Minat* = Coatzoacoalcos and Minatitlán.

Supply to the *colonias populares* is the responsibility of a specific department and differs from the system of provision to the city as a whole. A cheaper method of overland supply is used, whereas most other areas are provided by more expensive underground lines. The Electriticy Company also receives a government subsidy to cover 50% of the installation costs to these settlements. Selection of *colonias* to be supplied with a service is carried out wholly by the Company. Broadly, two criteria are important: first, the Company insists that approximately 60% of the plots should be occupied; and secondly, that the settlement be reasonably well laid out and that dwellings be made of permanent materials. Legal title is not required, and the purpose of the two stipulations is to minimize the risk of the Electricity Company installing a service only to find that the settlement is subsequently bulldozed out of existence. The programme of electricity provision is drawn up at three-monthly intervals and submitted to the DDF for approval. In practice the DDF 'rubber stamps' the list. Settlements get on to the list in a variety of ways: the Company carries out its own surveys, residents petition the Company, or requests come in from politicians or from high-level government officials. There is little scope for politicians, community groups or other government departments to prevent a settlement from receiving a service. Two survey settlements (Liberales and Jardines de Tepeyac) were supplied despite opposition from the *delegado* and municipal president respectively. The Electricity Company enjoys considerable autonomy from political interference.

The provision of street lighting, on the other hand, is subject to 'political' considerations. In this case the local authority decides which settlements are to receive the service. They pay the Company to install the service and later recover costs from individual households. Thus, settlements such as the two mentioned above were systematically denied public lighting because of their conflict with local authority officials. However, while most residents would not refuse the service if it were offered, it was rarely one of their top priorities.

Water and drainage provision
The provision of water and drainage both nationally and in Mexico City is much less widely available than electricity. Overall in 1980 almost one-third of dwellings in the Metropolitan Area lacked an interior water supply, although approximately one-half of these households did have access to a piped supply outside the dwelling – usually in the same plot. At a national level, and in most other cities, provision is not as widespread as in the capital (Table 5.1). The record for dwellings without a drainage system appears to be better, but this figure relates primarily to the broad definition of what constitutes a drainage system under the Mexican Census (a 'hygienic system for the removal of waste waters'; see Table 5.1).

Significantly, too, there is marked spatial variation nationally in the level of service provision. Broadly, rural areas are less well served than urban centres. State capitals appear to be better off than other large urban centres, while cities in the poorest regions such as the south and west (states such as Oaxaca, Chiapas and Guerrero) are poorly served (Table 5.1). The domestic coverage of a water supply in the rapidly expanding oil producing cities such as Coatzoacoalcos and Tampico deteriorated between 1970 and 1980, in contrast with the national trend. There are also marked variations between levels of service provision within cities. Those areas in Mexico City with extensive irregular settlement experience the highest levels of relative deprivation.

However, although adequate drainage and interior water supply is still lacking in many settlements, it would be churlish not to note the significant improvements registered since 1970. Both nationally and in the Metropolitan Area the number of dwellings provided with an interior supply of water and possessing a drainage system doubled between 1970 and 1980: a considerable achievement. This contributed to the relative improvement in servicing levels that is apparent in Table 5.1. Yet it is also important to recognize that, despite this investment, in absolute terms the position in 1980 was actually worse than a decade before. In 1980 there were more dwellings without an interior supply of running water than in 1970. The same feature appears in relation to dwellings with a drainage system, with the exception of the Metropolitan Area of Mexico City which had approximately the same number of dwellings unserviced as a decade earlier.

Neither do these figures tell us anything about the quality of the service. Without a purifier water is not, strictly speaking, drinkable. Most Mexico City residents who can afford it buy purified water in bottles or flagons. Also, the water supply itself is often irregular. During the dry season a common feature of water provision to some of the survey settlements was the irregularity with which it flowed. In Santo Domingo, for example, residents complained that the authorities may as well not have bothered to install a domestic supply as water flowed only in the early hours of the morning and was rarely sufficient to fill their tanks. Similarly, in many settlements in Netzahualcóyotl and Ecatepec, where water and drainage networks were installed during the mid-1970s, the drainage system has broken down. Subsequent urbanization works and heavy traffic have ruptured pipes; inadequate maintenance means that many drains are choked; and the lack of water means that wastes within the system are not flushed clear.

Given these failings we must treat the substantial improvements achieved between 1970 and 1980 with a degree of caution. Nevertheless, compared with conditions recorded in Mexico City during the 1960s and with those of other contemporary urban centres, it is apparent that Mexico City has been relatively favoured under recent investment programmes. In the discussion which follows I describe the nature of water and drainage provision in the city and evaluate the rationale underpinning the response by state authorities since 1970.

The bureaucracy responsible for water procurement and supply to domestic households is rather more complicated than in the case of electricity. More agencies are involved and although they operate in a technical manner there is an important distinction to be made between the bureaucratic system designed to procure the water to meet Mexico City's needs, and that which supplies water and drainage to individual households. The latter is rather more open to partisan political influence.

There are three broad levels of bureaucracy for water provision. Nationally, responsibility has changed hands between different government ministries (SARH before 1977, SAHOP between 1977 and 1983, and SEDUE from 1983). A regional commission (CAVM) is responsible for water procurement for Mexico City and beyond, and sells water both to the Federal District and the State of Mexico. Within the Federal District the water agency also sinks its own wells to supplement supplies.

The image and behaviour of the water agencies – the General Directorate of Construction and Water Operations (DGCOH) in the Federal District, and the State Commission for Water and Drainage (CEAS) in the State of Mexico – is broadly technical. Both have developed this image through their ability to provide a regular water supply to the city, through the manner in which they carry out their activities and by the stability of their personnel. In the Federal District the water agency (DGCOH), which before 1977 comprised two directorates – one for water procurement (DGOH), the other for supply (DGAyS) – has always enjoyed large budgets. Between 1971 and 1974 when the deep drainage system was being built something like 20% of the total Federal District expenditure and a much higher proportion of investment capital went to these agencies. At that time the large investment programme was an outcome of the demands made primarily by commercial and industrial companies in Mexico City for a good water supply. We have argued that both here and in Bogotá, efficiency and stability have been demanded of the water agency by the need to manage such large budgets (Gilbert & Ward 1985).

In Mexico City evidence of this efficiency and stability is not difficult to demonstrate. First, the agency successfully supplied most of the business needs of the city despite the speed of urban growth. Secondly, agency personnel have not changed as regularly as in other government offices: the head of the DGAyS, for example, remained in office from 1954 until his death in 1978, and then his long-standing deputy took over.

In supplying domestic consumers the DGCOH and its predecessors have tried to develop technical routines for the distribution of water. Here, however, the agency is more vulnerable to directives from politicians, notably from the president or the mayor who ultimately control expenditure. The latter decide the sort of service the agency is to provide and the broad priorities that are established. Occasionally, they intervene directly to solve the problems of particular settlements but this is exceptional, and normal practice is for the agency to act autonomously and to interpret in a technical way the guidelines imposed by politicians.

The priority which different administrations have given to the supply of water and drainage to low-income settlements has varied markedly. Prior to 1977, servicing provision to *colonias populares* in the Federal District was given low priority largely because the primary and secondary networks were incomplete. Nor could the agency take the initiative because there was no mechanism whereby it could recover the costs directly from consumers. Since investment had to come from the ordinary budget and was recovered by the Treasury under a separate account, any commitment to servicing the poor required a major budget increase to the agency. Because additional appropriations were not provided by the DDF to supply low-income areas, servicing continued on a rather *ad hoc* basis.

Earlier, during the 1960s, Mayor Uruchurtu had responded to public pressure and relaxed the requirement that irregular settlements be legalized before services could be provided. His successor continued and extended the practice and service provision, like land regularization, became linked to the process of political patronage: those settlements with close links to top government officials were most likely to receive some sort of service (Cornelius 1975). These officials would sometimes exert pressure on the agency. When the directive came from the president or the mayor then the settlement was usually serviced. Yet officials from the water agencies argued that they responded sympathetically to all settlement requests and tried to resist pressures that would result in queue jumping.

Nevertheless, during Echeverría's presidency, when popular mobilization and petitioning was strongly encouraged and when a large proportion of the agency's expenditure was directed towards the deep drainage programme, few low-income areas were adequately served. Rather, a 'holding' operation was initiated and those settlements designated for servicing were usually chosen because of their political contacts. Yet the service was often inadequate and consisted of hastily installed public standpipes or a supply delivered from water lorries. Both methods were inefficient and costly. Standpipes led to a lot of water being lost, and because it was not an individual supply no charge was levied. Water lorries were grossly inefficient: in 1973, 1000 litres of water delivered by lorry cost between 40 and 60 pesos, while the cost of an equivalent piped supply was only three pesos. The agency could act only as efficiently as the circumstances permitted.

In 1977, new policies were introduced to improve the efficiency and coverage of the supply to low-income neighbourhoods. The agencies' internal structure was reorganized and certain water and drainage functions were delegated to the local mayors. The Federal District Water Plan identified those areas lacking an adequate service and proposed to provide 1.2 million people with domestic water and 2 million with drainage by the end of 1982. Since 1977, decisions about the distribution of water to domestic users rest with the *delegado*. Through its overall control of financing, the agency obliges *delegados* to extend their network, to recover costs and to encourage community involvement in public works, but, as we shall observe below, the *delegado* has acquired considerable influence over the ordering of settlement priorities for service provision. As in the case of street lighting described earlier, in effect this means that politicial administrators determine who gets water. Of course the *delegado* receives technical advice and feasibility studies from his own engineers, but his final decision cannot be wholly based upon technical criteria. Of primary concern to the *delegado* is the maintenance of stability and control and the avoidance of upsurges of public protest. He is likely to accommodate political criteria alongside the technical advice that he receives from his subordinates. A settlement is likely to receive speedy attention where it is compliant with the *delegado*'s view, presses hard for services, and where the costs of installation are not prohibitively expensive. A weakly organized or non-compliant settlement may well be dropped off the programme agenda, especially if it would be costly to service.

Therefore, although the operations of the water agency continue to be governed primarily by technical criteria, there is considerable opportunity for partisan rationality on matters concerned with domestic supply. In many ways the role of the DGCOH has become rather similar to the traditional role of the technical agencies higher up the water procurement ladder. Like the CAVM, the role is one of providing the water and extending the primary network in order to get it to the distributors lower down the order.

In the State of Mexico, water and drainage are the responsibility of a special commission created in 1973 (CEAS). Established with Federal funds to help overcome the social unrest in Netzahualcóyotl and Ecatepec during the early 1970s, it had installed services to most settlements by 1978. Costs were being recovered from residents over a ten-year period. It was staffed by trained officials who are responsible to the governor. In theory, CEAS should sell water to the municipality which is responsible for the supply and sale to residents; in practice, however, the municipality is too small a unit to have the necessary resources and personnel, so CEAS takes responsibility. In this respect, municipal intervention is less marked than that of their approximate counterparts (the *delegaciones*) within the Federal District.

Water and drainage provision in Mexico City, therefore, is predominantly technical with respect to water procurement and to the supply of business and industrial users. Water and drainage are essential if these sectors are to help maintain economic growth. As a consequence the water authorities receive high priority in government budgets. For those residential sectors that can afford to pay for their water there is no difficulty in being served: norms, charges and procedures are all clearly laid down by the agency and strictly followed. The poor, however, do not fall into this category. Whether they are serviced depends on the political priority given to satisfying their needs and to the pressures that local groups exert on the government. The agency continues to act in a technically responsible way, but political rationality becomes more influential. In the case of water supply politicians influence the priorities much more than in the case of electricity.

The influence of community mobilization for service provision

In the previous chapter I concluded that the state used its influence over land resources as a primary means to manipulate and control the poor. The growing technocratic style of the state was exemplified by recent policies towards land regularization which act to integrate the poor into the fiscal and planning framework. The question here is does the same argument apply in the case of urban servicing? The discussion so far has suggested that the bureaucracies responsible for water and drainage are far more autonomous and technically rational in fulfilling their functions than those involved in land regularization.

In the following section I want to identify the extent to which community mobilization determines service provision. Do people mobilize to lobby and petition government agencies and politicians? If so to what purpose, given that servicing is supposedly a routine technical matter? To what extent, and how, does the state use the resources of water and electricity as a medium for ensuring social stability and working-class compliance with its policies? What are the channels of communication and interaction between the state and the local community, and how do they function?

The extent of community mobilization for services

Community participation in local development projects is widely regarded as valuable. The argument is that people know best what they want and are likely to show greater commitment to projects if they reflect their expressed needs rather than the views of planners (Martin 1983). Participation has other advantages: it foments democracy, and provides opportunities for individuals to gain experience as leaders (United Nations 1970, Skinner 1983). It may significantly reduce the costs of public works and, therefore, benefit the poor. It may also provide opportunities for governments and politicians to exercise greater control over the grassroots who become involved through community participation (Skinner 1983).

In Mexico there is a long tradition since Precolumbian times of community works carried out by the public. In many rural parts of the country a *tequio* system operates which involves families giving up the equivalent of a day's labour to assist in local public works. Often in recently formed irregular settlements neighbours collaborate in *faenas* to open up vehicular access, install illegal electricity hook-ups, and to construct community buildings. Usually these activities are organized collectively on a Sunday morning. Recent policies have attempted to capitalize on these experiences of community labour and to institutionalize them in local development projects.[2]

The stimulus to organize collectively usually comes from below. It may arise from the nature of land acquisition, particularly in the case of invasions which require careful planning beforehand, and families may be 'screened' by leaders who decide whether or not they can join. Alternatively, an organization may form in response to a crisis: a threat to evict residents, for example. It may also arise as a practical response both to defend the community and to seek benefits on its behalf. Residents' associations, therefore, are common throughout Mexican irregular settlements, as they are elsewhere in Latin America. However, they are not always formally constituted. Often they comprise loose arrangements of followers organized around a particular leader, or around factions if the settlement is riven with different leaders in competition with one another.

In contrast, the existence of a formal association with a constitution, rules and elected representatives is generally stimulated from above and is an expression of the influence of supra-local authorities rather than an outcome of the wishes of the people themselves. Thus, the formal association in Isidro Fabela which formed in 1964 was encouraged by the then Oficina de Colonias, itself a thinly disguised mobilizing agent for the CNOP wing of the PRI. Much more recently, after 1977, many settlements formally constituted their existing arrangements once the DDF identified the *juntas de vecinos* as the primary route through which services were to be negotiated. A similar arrangement existed in the State of Mexico with the Consejos de Colaboración.[3] Formal community associations only tend to emerge where the city-wide rules of 'petitioning' demand it.

The extent to which people are likely to take community action to demand services and settlement improvements varies according to age of settlement, its size, the heterogeneity of tenure and income groups within it, and the attributes of its leaders (Gilbert & Ward 1985). Above all, the degree to which the government cultivates active petitioning as a pre-requisite to servicing is likely to determine participation. In this respect Mexico has a tradition of encouraging structured, controlled political contact by citizens – more than any other Latin American country with the possible exception of Cuba, as Fagen and Tuohy argue (1972: 88–9). Certainly in our comparison of community participation in Colombia, Venezuela and Mexico, Mexico emerged as the one in which owner households were most likely to have been active in some way or other.[4]

After land regularization, the issues around which households most commonly mobilized in Mexico were water and electricity (Table 5.2). By comparison school facilities and health centres were less likely to provide a focus for action. This reflects the priorities accorded each item by low-income households: regularization is first because it relates to security of continued occupancy; water and electricity because they are the two services that residents feel they can least do without. But are resident mobilization, forceful leadership and good links with the political and governmental bureaucracy necessary for settlements to win urban services? Clearly they are, otherwise very few people would become involved. Yet I shall argue below that the significance of these activities in determining contemporary allocation of resources between settlements is probably marginal.

Table 5.2 Participation levels among owner-occupiers by settlement (percentages).

	Isidro Fabela	Santo Domingo los Reyes	El Sol	Liberales	Chalma Guadalupe	Jardines de Tepeyac
owner households' participation						
land regularization	36	50	29	96	33	44
installation of electricity	24	26	20	70	22	28
installation of water	24	34	12	60	31	33
school facilities	12	19	15	29	7	19
health centre	3	5	5	6	0	1
(total number of replies)	(90)	(97)	(84)	(47)	(54)	(75)
principal participant						
no one	47	36	53	4	53	35
male head or husband	60	33	57	32	56	56
female head or wife	18	38	22	20	16	4
male and female jointly	22	29	21	48	28	40
(total number of participants)	(45)	(58)	(37)	(44)	(25)	(48)
participation in a residents' association						
never	66	78	77	4	82	68
constantly involved	8	14	6	92	11	19
involved mostly in past	26	7	17	2	8	5
involved mostly in present	0	0	0	2	0	8
(total number of participants)	(85)	(97)	(84)	(48)	(54)	(75)
total number of households interviewed	(144)	(120)	(120)	(60)	(73)	(114)

Source
PIHLU survey, 1979.

Channels for community action and their impact, 1970–84

Prior to 1970 when the Federal District began to make concerted use of a single organizational channel for government–community interaction, there was no formal structure. Unlike many Latin American governments Mexico had not been stimulated by the Alliance for Progress into creating a department for 'community participation' – at least not formally.[5] In Mexico the authorities preferred to handle community – state relations through existing institutions. If those proved inadequate they could be replaced or duplicated. From the government's point of view the perceived danger was that a single structure that sought to integrate low-income communities under one umbrella might constitute a major threat. It would heighten the chances of horizontal linkages forming between settlements: anathema to the Mexican political system, especially after the experience of the MRC in Netzahualcóyotl where the state was forced to demobilize an incipient social movement (Ward 1981a: 388).

Therefore, the approach adopted was one of carefully wrought patron–client links with individual settlements. Community leaders were encouraged to act as 'brokers' between those whom they represented – the residents – and those from whom they sought assistance – the 'patrons' (see Grindle 1977: 42–5). A patron may be a politician, a high-ranking government functionary, the mayor or even the national president. In return for the residents' support, the patron seeks to assist the local community.

This structure of 'mutual benefit' has two important implications. First, it welds a form of social relation which makes the poor subservient to, and dependent upon, more powerful individuals. Thus resources cannot be demanded or negotiated as of right: they must be exchanged for political support, for good behaviour and compliance with those in authority. In short, services may become a crucial part in the system of patronage. For the Mexican state, or for those who are in the position of dominance and can manipulate this support, the system offers obvious advantages. A second implication is that those who control the outflow of resources are able to slow down the overall rate at which the system meets demands made upon it. Negotiation through a large number of patrons takes time, and there is an informal limit to the rate at which demands may be made of a patron. In this way the government manages to curtail 'demands for expensive, generalized benefits that might "overload" the political system' (Cornelius 1975: 160).

There are other ways in which the state exercises control over the population, notably the co-option of leaders (Eckstein 1977: 100) and, occasionally, through violent repression and/or the assassination of leaders (Montaño 1976, Ugalde et al. 1974). But in the context of Mexico City patron–clientelism has traditionally provided the most frequently used medium of control.

Between 1971 and 1976 President Echeverría used patron–client links to generate broad support from low-income groups who could be mobilized to attend speeches, rallies, and visits of dignatories. As we have observed in Chapter 4, several new agencies were established in order to generate close contact with local leaders and to attend to their demands. The president, too, opened his door to petitions and lobbying from communities, thereby encouraging them to bypass the appropriate authorities.

The impact that this structure of community mobilization had in determining which settlements were serviced presents something of a paradox. Certainly those residents who organized, shouted loudest, made a nuisance of themselves and had good contacts within the government were most likely to receive attention. But, with the important exception of Netzahualcóyotl, the services on offer were very partial – the arrival of a water lorry (the *pipa*), communal standpipes and so on. Thus although mobilization was important, the fruits likely to be won from it were limited: hence the paradox.

The political and ideological benefits of this process of resource allocation are quite clear. It provided maximum flexibility of political control: the president could modify agency programmes, create new agencies, and confer or withdraw support to groups and individuals. He was also able to keep a close check on the effectiveness of his appointees and kept them under the same sort of work pressure that he himself sustained. By creating the facility for the proliferation of local groups and by encouraging their informal links with a variety of patrons, he ensured a personal backing that could be employed to support his policies when he came under political pressure at different points throughout his administration. Ultimately, too, he could take personal charge of any major upsurge of unrest.

In 1977 an initiative of the new mayor, Hank González, caused the role of community mobilization for services to change quite dramatically. Patron–client links declined in importance and were replaced by a more technocratic structure of community mobilization. This arose in part because the process of decentralization of many servicing functions, begun under Echeverría, was hastened under the new administration. Responsibility for street paving, street lighting, water and drainage provision came under the purview of local mayors (delegados). The latter were given larger though quite inadequate budgets and were left to draw up priorities for servicing the communities in their areas and to submit plans annually to the Federal District central departments. In this way the city mayor continued to control resources but created a method for determining servicing priorities which deflected attention away from himself and the new president, and towards his appointees, the delegados. The 'open door' of the previous administration was quietly closed and any settlement leader who mistakenly led his followers to the central offices was sent to his local delegado.

The new channel of community–state negotiations was created by breathing life into an existing (but largely unused) structure called the juntas de vecinos. Each settlement elected local association representatives (jefes de manzana), one of whom was elected community president. He or she represented the community at the delegación level on the junta de vecinos, the function of which was to report and advise on settlement servicing, to participate in civic occasions and to comment on housing, social services and administration. They had no executive functions (Mexico DDF 1979). The junta elected one of its members to be president and to serve on a city-wide Consultative Council. In practice most of those who served on the pre-1980 juntas were nominated by the delegado and this led to widespread dissent among local groups who found themselves excluded. In 1980 and 1983, however, considerable effort and expense was spent by the DDF authorities to ensure democratic, 'apolitical' elections and to encourage active involvement in them.

These juntas were given power as a result of the instructions which Mayor Hank González gave to delegados to ensure that, for negotiation purposes, they recognize only those leaders legitimately elected to the junta. Further, the business of selecting priorities and programmes for service and other provision to local settlements was to be decided, at least in part, by the junta de vecinos. Members of each delegación junta met once a month with top functionaries of the DDF.[6] This meeting provided the opportunity for elected representatives of residents' associations to complain about local problems and to submit requests for supplementary funding of an urgent nature that could not be accommodated through the normal budgetary procedure of annual appropriations to the *delegado*.

The adoption of an institutionalized structure for community organization and servicing – in this case water provision and street lighting – has several important implications for the degree of social control exercised by the government. The *junta* structure has increased the control which the *delegado* exercises over the local populace, which is arguably greater than that achieved by earlier patron–client methods. The *delegado* is more autonomous and has greater authority to determine local improvement programmes than before. Moreover, decisions are taken in collaboration with the *junta* so that negotiation and competition between settlements effectively shifts responsibility away from the *delegado* and the central agencies and places the onus upon local neighbourhoods to sort out their own problems. The issue becomes one of how to divide the cake rather than how much cake is put on the table.

The city mayor also benefits. He has been able to devolve to *delegados* many of the pressures and responsibilities associated with demand making from low-income communities. Yet his power is not diminished as he retains close control over resources through annual budgets, and he is able to sustain contact with the grassroots through regular monthly meetings undertaken by his staff. In the event of any local crisis he can take *ad hoc* action through the *junta*. Ideologically, too, the *juntas* help instil the concept of 'good citizenship', a catchword used by several top officials whom I interviewed. Low-income residents have a responsibility to pay for services they receive, to pay their taxes, to conserve water and not to drop litter. Thus community mobilization is identified with 'apolitical' civic issues and invokes less radical rhetoric about the rights of the poor and their class struggle.

Since 1982 it has also become apparent that the *juntas* fulfil an important political role in providing an alternative to a widely voiced demand that the headship of the DDF (and, one assumes, the local mayors) be elected in the same way as state governors and municipal presidents elsewhere. During the 1982 federal elections there were numerous calls from both the PRI and opposition parties for an elected local congress and for elected officials and chief administrators (*Proceso*, 14 May 1982). Similarly, during the *Consulta Popular* carried out in 1983 many of the same groups repeated their arguments (*Unomásuno*, 24 March 1983). Opposition parties, particularly those on the left, have much of their power base within the capital and could be optimistic of winning considerable, if not overall, executive influence within the District. The PRI are in favour of elected representatives because they feel that it would give their deputies greater access to resources that could be used for political patronage. For the government, however, the sensitivity of this area – the president's 'backyard' – makes it a potentially dangerous and unthinkable proposition. The mayor's response was that the proposal would be studied carefully by the Federal District Department and recommendations would be put to the Plenary sessions of the *Consulta Popular*, organised by the Interior Ministry. In effect he was putting the proposal on the back burner.

Thus the *junta de vecinos* in its 'apolitical' form offers a key counter-argument to the need for an 'elected' Federal District executive: elected representatives already exist. The important matter for government is to demonstrate that a sufficient proportion of the populace can be shown to have participated in the *junta* 'elections'. The government's attempt to sustain the legitimacy of the *junta* structure perforce threatens to alienate PRI interests which cannot be overtly accommodated if the apolitical symbolism of the *juntas* is to be maintained. In the 1983 elections the authorities were very sensitive to accusations that the PRI was actively involved in the process of *junta* elections. It was yet another indication of the growing strain between the governmental and political bureaucracies in Mexico.

The costs of service installation

But can the poor afford the costs of service installation? Have these costs become more or less expensive in real terms? Does receipt of a formal level of servicing significantly raise the weekly or monthly outgoings that the poor are obliged to pay? Is the phasing of repayments and consumption charges appropriate within the context of low incomes and self-build housing options? Answers to these questions are important if we are to determine the economic pressures imposed upon the poor as a result of government intervention on their behalf.

Both water and electricity provision are heavily subsidized. We have already observed that the government provides a 50% subsidy for the costs of electricity provision to *colonias populares*, and that instead of an underground cable supply a cheaper overhead service is provided. Similarly in the case of water provision it is estimated that between 1969 and 1979 only about one-quarter of the total investment in water and drainage costs was recovered from one-off charges and from repetitive charges to the public (Makin 1984: 286). Broadly, installation costs are not prohibitively expensive, as a combination of subsidy and government policy not to insist on full cost recovery reduces prices to a level that makes them affordable to most of the poor. Electricity is the cheaper of the two services, costing, on average, between 1000 and 2000 pesos at 1978 values (Table 5.3). My findings are corroborated by those of Chant (1984) in Querétaro and by Varley (1985) in Mexico City, although in the latter prices appear to be somewhat higher for local reasons.[7] Expressed as a proportion of monthly income of household heads the costs of electricity installation do not appear to be especially onerous, the total cost fluctuating between one-quarter and one-half of a single month's wages.

The costs of water installation are more variable (Table 5.3). Costs appear to vary according to the nature of the service provided, the ease of installation, plot size and the strength with which leaders protested the settlement's 'popular'

Table 5.3 Installation costs of water and electricity service by individual settlements in Mexico City (1978 pesos).

Settlement[a]	Electricity			Water		
	Year	Mode	Mean	Year	Mode	Mean
Isidro Fabela	1971	1170	1300	1978	2000	1693
El Sol[b]	1975	880	1177	1975	15800	8386
Santo Domingo los Reyes	1978	1100	1210	1978	2000	2017
Jardines de Tepeyac[c]	1971	1760	1844	1977	2700	3161
Liberales	1979	2110	1777	no service in 1979		
Chalma Guadalupe	1974	810	1090	no service in 1979		

Source
PIHLU survey, 1979.
Notes
According to the same survey the average monthly income of the head of household expressed in 1978 values was 4163 pesos. Average household incomes were somewhat higher, at 4748 pesos.

[a] The mode and mean values were calculated for the year in which the largest number of households received the service in each settlement.
[b] Includes drainage. This charge forms part of the so-called 'special deal' negotiated in Netzahualcóyotl. Households paid 9000 pesos (1975 prices), with repayments over ten years.
[c] Higher values here probably reflect the presence of larger plot sizes. Calculations do not take into account plot size.

status. They also appear to be higher in the State of Mexico. For example, in 1976–7 proposals to charge residents 27 000 pesos for water and drainage for 550 square metre plots in Jardines de Tepeyac were resisted by settlement leaders. Noteworthy, too, are the relatively high prices paid by residents of El Sol, where a comprehensive service was provided in 1975. This formed part of the 'special deal' established by the government for the *colonias* of Netzahualcóyotl once it had taken over responsibility from the real-estate developers. Usually, however, the cost of a domestic water supply comprising a small-bore connection from the street a few metres on to the plot was between 2000 and 3000 (1978) pesos. These costs appear to have remained broadly static in real terms – at least up until 1979 when my survey data end. Chant's (1984) findings for Querétaro suggest that electricity prices have not increased in real terms during 1980–2.

Repetitive costs that arise from service installation
It is important to evaluate the outgoings incurred by low-income households once they become consumers. As we have observed, water charges are assessed at a flat rate while electricity is paid for according to the number of units consumed.

Few studies have made a serious attempt to quantify the expenditure on services by low-income households in irregular settlements. One estimate

(Bazant 1979) combines repayments for water and electricity installation and consumption costs and suggests that households spend somewhere between 435 and 470 pesos a month at 1978 prices. Referring to electricity consumption alone, Bazant estimated (*ibid*. 161) a monthly expenditure of between 53 and 88 pesos. Two recent studies which collected data about household budgets and servicing (Chant 1984, Varley 1985) have been made available to me, and two points emerge from them. First, the monthly charges for water and electricity (actually assessed bimonthly in Mexico) are relatively low. Electricity costs roughly 60-70 pesos a month in 1978 values; while water works out at around 100 pesos. The second feature is an indication of the costs of services incurred by low-income families before they receive a formal network. For example, water must be bought either from the *pipa* (notwithstanding that it is supposedly a free service) or from water vendors. If electricity is stolen then there are costs involved in the purchase of cable. More usually households spend considerable amounts on alternative sources of lighting (candles and kerosene lamps). Chant's data show that these costs are likely to be considerably higher than a formal regular supply – a point also noted by Makin (1984: 287).

Obviously much depends upon how contributions towards installation costs are collected. If they are demanded in a one-off payment *(al contado)* then the amount may be difficult to raise and hardship may result. However, assuming that repayments are allowed over a three year period, an average sized plot with installation costs of (1978) 1500 pesos for electricity and 2500 pesos for water (common round-figure estimates drawn from the PIHLU data), the monthly repayment would be 111 pesos. Add to this 170 pesos for consumption costs and the sum appears to be no more than that paid for 'informal' services. Nevertheless, taking into account average incomes of heads of household in the survey settlements this sum represents around 7% of the monthly wage – a not insignificant amount.[8] Moreover, to return to the point made earlier, the installation of a domestic water supply does not mean that water is available all year round. Residents may find that for some part of the year they are obliged to buy water informally, while at the same time paying for an ineffective household connection. The important point to recognize here is that, taken individually, the costs of service installation and consumption do not appear to be onerous, nor do they appear to have increased in real terms over the last decade and a half.

The overall costs of irregular settlement residence: an affordable 'solution'?
So far I have analysed costs for individual items – land acquisition, and the installation and consumption costs of water and electricity. The conclusion that I have drawn is that, individually, these costs do not appear to be particularly high, nor have they increased greatly in real terms over the past decade and a half. However, two other considerations must be taken into account. First, there are other costs that may also make serious demands upon household incomes. Second, costs associated with residence in irregular settlement may

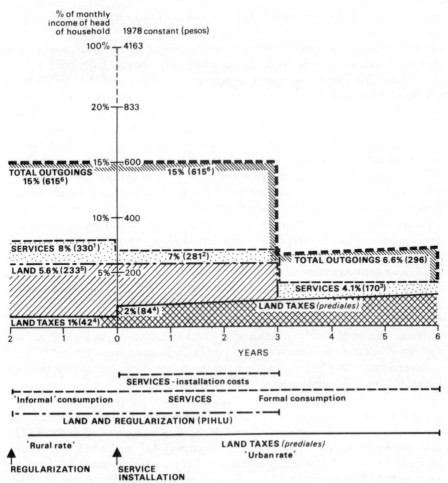

Figure 5.1 The costs of residence in irregular settlement at different phases of development.

Notes

1 Estimate taken from Chant (1984).
2 As described in the text, this includes estimated monthly consumption payments (water and electricity of 170 (1978) pesos, and 'installation' charges of 111 pesos per month. Source is the PIHLU survey.
3 Source as for note 2. Consumption payments of 170 pesos.
4 Makin (1984: 304–24). *Impuestos prediales* are calculated from the cadastral value of the land. Although the latter takes account of dwelling structures the curve in Fig 5.1 is based upon land values only. In reality, taxes are likely to be 20–30% higher than the level shown.
5 As I note in the text this total monthly repayment is likely to be an underestimate. It includes an estimate for land costs calculated from the average price of lots as given in the PIHLU survey. Had I taken the highest land prices recorded in the irregular settlements (El Sol), with repayments calculated over five years, then the total would have been around 25% of the monthly head of household's income.
6 A conservative estimate of the total outgoings for land, land taxes, and services.

not be phased in a manner that allows repayments to be made over a long period of time: 'bottlenecks' may occur during which costs are especially high.

In Figure 5.1 I have attempted to portray the phasing of charges likely to accrue in relation to land acquisition and servicing in irregular settlements in Mexico City. Two sets of payments appear: one-off charges which may, in fact, be spread over several years; and charges for consumption or occupancy in the case of land taxes. The amount of each of these charges is shown on the y-axis expressed in 1978 pesos and as a proportion of average monthly income of head of household. I have assumed that services begin to be installed two years after land regularization has begun, and that the lump sum costs paid by owners are paid over three years; also that 'urban' land taxes begin to be paid from about the time that formal services begin to be installed.[9] In reality, of course, regularization may take place several years earlier, or, indeed, may be concurrent with servicing. In calculating the costs I have used broad 'average' figures described above and derived from our sample survey in 1979. But, as we saw earlier and on Table 5.3, these costs vary between settlements, especially for items such as land prices and water installation. However, at the level of generalization with which I am concerned it will provide a useful idea of overall costs and their phasing. We may safely assume that the sums shown in Figure 5.1 are conservative estimates: in practice they are likely to be higher.

Several important points emerge from the figure. First, we can see how the period in which the combination of one-off charges and consumption costs are likely to be greatest occurs in the immediate pre- and post-servicing phase, particularly when repayments for land acquisition and servicing overlap. At this time it is likely that at least 15% of the head of household's income will be absorbed by those costs. The problem is compounded by the frequent practice by the authorities of demanding additional charges which come precisely at this time, with little opportunity to spread payments over two or three years. These include back payments of up to five years' *predial* taxes; fines for not registering construction plans with the appropriate offices and surcharges relating to non-payment of previous taxes. Although when taken individually these sums appear small, coming at this moment in the phasing of repayments they can cause real hardship. Secondly, there is little apparent difference in outgoings in the pre-servicing and post-servicing phase, a result of the considerable drain on resources that informally acquired services are estimated to represent. If there is little effective difference in the cost of the two systems then most households may be expected to welcome initiatives to install a formal supply. Thirdly, there is a very sharp decline in outgoings (from around 15% to 6.6% of the head of household's wage per month) once the one-off payments are completed. Although this decline may be exaggerated in Figure 5.1 in that I have assumed that repayments for land, regularization and servicing finish at the same time, in practice there is unlikely to be a major time lapse. Usually repayments for one-off items are concluded within a year or two of each other.

This 'bottleneck' in the costs of irregular settlement may have important repercussions upon the residential 'mix', that is, the economic heterogeneity of households living within the settlement. Significant hardship is likely to be experienced by some families during a relatively short phase of the settlement's development. The very poor (i.e. those earning less than the minimum wage) face major and inflexible monthly repayments and must either sell out or attempt to meet these additional costs in some other way. This might include sharing the costs with other household members, sharing their plot with kin, or renting out a portion of it. Alternatively, the relatively high commercial value that the plot now commands may persuade them to cash in and move elsewhere (Ward 1982b, Makin 1984). Other households, even though their wages are higher, may also seek to spread the impact of the costs in a similar manner.

Another important outcome of high outgoings during the period of state intervention is the slowing down of the rate of settlement improvement. The cash surplus which households would usually hope to use in 'self-help' or 'self-managed' dwelling improvements associated with successful 'consolidation' may be significantly eroded by the spate of charges that come as a result of government intervention on behalf of the community. The double irony is that once the costs of land purchase and service installation are paid, periodic charges fall away quite dramatically and would, theoretically, allow even the poorest to survive in self-help settlements. Yet, by that time, for some households it will be too late.

Conclusion

This chapter has demonstrated, perhaps more clearly than any other, the way in which the Mexican state is becoming more technocratic in its approach and the effect that this is having upon the poor. In the case of two services – water and electricity – we have observed that agency behaviour and performance is much more 'technical' in contrast to their counterparts in land, housing and health provision. They enjoy considerable autonomy from state interference, have large budgets and stability of personnel, most of whom are appointed on the basis of technical qualifications rather than their affiliation to power groups within Mexican society. The key difference between these agencies and others analysed in this book is their primary significance in contributing to production and economic growth. More than anything else this explains their consistently high budgets and the technical routines by which they run. Put simply, the government could not afford to have them to fail or be run inefficiently, as manufacturing, business and commerce are dependent upon them. Once on line, priority is given to ensuring that the rich and middle-income groups are adequately and efficiently served. This also heads off any threat of political embarrassment that might otherwise beset the government.

Increasingly, the same is true of supplying the poor, even though they come at the end of the queue. Once plentiful supplies of relatively cheap water and electricity are available and the needs of other users have been met, the government seeks to use provision as one of its primary means whereby it assists in the reproduction of labour. Both services are provided under heavy subsidies, and significant progress has been achieved in extending the supply to low-income groups, particularly in Mexico City and other large urban centres. The agencies responsible for servicing the poor are the same as those providing all other users: hence they attempt to operate in a 'technically rational' manner. By and large they are able to fulfil their duties without political interference even if they are not totally immune from such considerations. On the other hand domestic supply of water and drainage is more likely to be affected by political criteria because decisions about which settlements are to receive a service, and in what order, are made primarily by officials whose concern is not simply one of technical efficiency. Hence an important difference between rich and poor neighbourhoods is that the latter must mobilize to seek to persuade those officials to extend provision to their areas.

Community mobilization is an important first step towards servicing, but I have argued that, by itself, it does not determine successful outcomes. The latter is mostly a product of local government's commitment to make available the necessary resources for widespread provision. Within that framework poor communities must compete with one another. The channels that the government has adopted to manage that competition – whether through patron-clientelism or a hierarchical residents' association structure – have aimed to ensure compliance and social stability and to ensure that demand making does not exceed the limits of expenditure set by the state.

Because they are subsidized, the costs of water and electricity installation to low-income communities are usually at levels which make them affordable to 'owner' households in irregular settlements. Broadly those costs appear to have remained stable since the early 1970s. Consumption costs, also, are affordable to the poor. Indeed I have found that the 'informal' costs of acquiring water and power are often considerably more than a formal supply after installation. A recurrent problem, however, is that the water and drainage systems provided are unreliable or are inadequately maintained so that sometimes the poor must pay for both formal and informal methods of supply. Another problem is the way in which the costs of supply and consumption are recovered from irregular settlements. Although taken individually each item is affordable to most families, there is a short period in which these costs, together with repayments for land, regularization and sundry resultant taxes, become excessive. This may force families to sell up, or to adopt strategies that will allow them to meet the high levels of repayment. Whichever happens, unnecessary hardship and a slowing down of self-help activities to improve dwellings may result.

Notes

1   The reader is referred to an earlier version of this matrix, together with counterparts for Bogotá and Valencia, which appear in Gilbert and Ward (1985).

2 Recent policies established within both the Federal District and the State of Mexico have sought
   to encourage community participation and labour in local development projects. Specifically
   these comprise some public works in the *delegaciones* (notably Alvaro Obregón); the self-help
   schemes of the DEPROVI organized by AURIS; and the so-called volunteer 'work army'
   (Ejército de trabajo) promoted by Governor Jimenez Cantú.
3 The *consejos* were different in one important respect. They combined functions whereby local
   communities made representations to the municipality about local improvements, services, and
   so on, with the function of municipal authority within the settlement. Thus the job of some
   elected 'delegates' was to provide elementary policing in the neighbourhood, to report
   misconduct to the municipal president and so on. Usually two separate groups fulfilled each
   function, but they were elected on the same slate.
4 In Mexico around 60% of owner households reported that one or several members of their
   household had been involved in activities such as petitioning, attendance at community
   association meetings, or *faenas*. In contrast, this figure was considerably lower in Bogotá and
   Valencia (Gilbert & Ward 1985: 204).
5 For example in Colombia where Acción Comunal had existed since 1958; and in Venezuela
   where *juntas pro-mejoras* were established in the same year and consolidated by CORDIPLAN
   during the 1960s (Gilbert & Ward 1985). Similar arrangements appeared in Lima (Collier 1976).
6 The officials who most usually attended were the Government Secretary A (effectively second in
   command); a high-ranking member of the public works department; the chief planner and so on.
   The mayor himself did not normally attend these meetings.
7 I am grateful to Sylvia Chant and Ann Varley for kindly providing me with comparative data for
   the settlements in which they worked. The somewhat higher prices encountered in two of
   Varley's six study areas are due to the larger plot sizes in those settlements, the fact that street
   lighting was often included in the total price and by the apparent practice of withdrawing cheaper
   concessionary charges in middle-income sectors of irregular settlement.
8 Makin (1984: 287) derives a broadly similar sum in his calculations of payments for water and
   electricity. According to his estimates costs will amount to around 11% to 12% of the official
   minimum salary in 1980 terms. He notes that while these costs could be expected to decline once
   the one-off charges have been met (after 1–3 years), in fact they will remain broadly similar,
   being replaced by the higher land taxes.
9 One cost that has not yet been discussed in detail is the *boleta predial*. In essence these are taxes
   assessed upon the cadastral value of the land. Urban land is assessed at more than twice the rate of
   'rural' property. Taxes are levied bi-monthly and are broadly designed to contribute towards the
   services enjoyed in the settlement. Land taxes feature as an important element of Federal District
   fiscal policy. Although the overall significance of land taxes as a proportion of ordinary income
   of the DDF has declined from around 21% in the early 1970s to 12% a decade later, the absolute
   income has increased in real terms (Makin 1984: Table 5.10). In 1979 when I interviewed the then
   director of the cadastral office he confirmed that they were making a concerted effort to extend
   the *predial* tax net to cover irregular settlements. The subsequent impact of this policy is clearly
   seen: the number of plots registered for *predial* purposes rose from 804130 to 906652 between
   1978 and 1979 (an unprecedented 13% increase).

6   Health care and inequality

In this final substantive chapter I examine one of the most important dimensions of social welfare: that of health care. As in previous chapters proper understanding of this element of social welfare provision cannot be divorced from Mexico's political economy. Although medicine and health have often been analysed according to a narrow, purely biomedical perspective, recent studies have adopted a theoretical view whereby social, economic and political structures are the major determinants of the way in which health is perceived and treated (Eyles & Woods 1983). Disease is no longer conceived as an abnormality which requires the intervention of a qualified and scientifically neutral profession. Although the practice of medicine in many countries continues to be dominated by this approach, most research today sees health and medical care as intimately related to the society of which it forms a part. As such, medicine and health care are social issues which both reflect and, some would argue, are integral to the processes whereby societies reproduce themselves. Under capitalism health care forms part of the apparatus that facilitates the social reproduction process and social integration. It sustains capitalist relations between competing classes and it reduces dissent (Navarro 1974, 1978, Elling 1981). A less economically deterministic view emphasizes the ideological role that medical agencies play, and is primarily concerned with the 'societal effects and implications of the enmeshing of medicine/health care in the wider society' (Eyles & Woods 1983: 27).

This last-mentioned perspective has an important bearing upon the analysis of health care in Mexico. It suggests that we should not merely try to understand the health problems in Mexico as a technical matter in which total resources are inadequate or are inequitably distributed. Although this fact should not be ignored it is the underlying response to health that is important. Are governmental responses primarily curative or preventive and why? What role do health care delivery systems play in reproducing social relations and does access accentuate or reduce social inequality? What opportunities do health care policies offer for political manipulation?

Illness in Mexico

The accuracy of statistical data about mortality and morbidity patterns in Latin America leaves much to be desired. There is widespread underreporting and specified cause of death is notoriously inaccurate given that many deaths are not certified by a doctor. Therefore some countries may be considerably worse off than they appear from official statistics. Mexico has relatively good sources of information and accurate reporting so there may be some validity in the argument that statistics which place it at the worse end of the mortality and morbidity tables are partly a distortion brought about by its more assiduous reporting. Whatever the true ranking, there is clearly a major problem. Mexico shows a classic pattern of high birth rates and a rapidly declining death rate brought about by dramatic improvements in health care and immunization programmes since the Revolution. Overall its annual rate of population growth between 1960 and 1975 was 3.3% – consistently one of the highest in the world. Only recently has it begun to show significant signs of a downturn as a result of firm government commitment to population control measures from 1973 onwards. The Mexican Population Commission (CONAPO) established a policy in 1978 which planned to reduce growth from 3.2% to 2.1% by 1982, and to 1% by the end of the century. Although this is highly optimistic, and despite the fact that the 1982 target was not met, significant progress has been made in reducing natural increase. In 1984 the annual rate of growth was estimated at 2.3% (*People*, 11 March 1984: 6).

Certain types of illness are heavily represented in Mexican statistics and most are the direct outcome of poor environmental living conditions and poverty. Infant mortality is high, and low birthweight is more frequently encountered than in most developed countries. Deaths in children under five years are five times as high as those recorded in Cuba, Canada and the United States. Similarly, although less extreme, death rates for all other age groups are much higher than in the aforementioned countries (López Acuña 1980: 49). The principal causes of death are respiratory diseases such as bronchitis, tuberculosis, influenza and pneumonia, and infectious intestinal disorders such as enteritis and other diarrhoea-type illnesses. Typhoid, paratyphoid and other salmonella infections are also common. Mexico also appears to be a particularly violent country, with accidental deaths and homicides ranking very high (Fox 1972, López Acuña 1980). Conversely, compared to the USA and Canada, diseases traditionally associated with old age are much less frequent in Mexico. The important point is that a large proportion of the illnesses that figure so prominently in Mexico could be prevented, or at least dramatically reduced, with improved sanitation and housing conditions (López Acuña 1980: 92).

It is difficult to ascertain whether urban places are less healthy than rural districts because many rural deaths and illnesses are registered in towns or go unreported in the most isolated districts. In the Metropolitan Area high mortality and morbidity rates are associated with low-income areas and poor housing conditions (Fox 1972). Those living in the eastern suburbs of Netzahualcóyotl were especially prone to intestinal infections brought about by the poor sanitary and water supply conditions that existed in those areas – at least up until the early 1970s. Those living in the working-class neighbourhoods of Tepito and Guerrero in the heart of the city suffer excessively from respiratory diseases due to cramped housing conditions and high levels of pollution (Fox 1972). Overall, therefore, the general panorama is one of 'ill health, malnutrition and high rates of illness and death that are similar to those occasionally found in European countries at the early phase of the Industrial Revolution. Urgently required is an analysis of national health programmes in the light of the real problems encountered by the population' (López Acuña 1980: 94).

This brief overview of the nature of ill health in Mexico underlines the need for community health programmes that concentrate upon preventive medicine. Improved water and drainage supplies, higher nutritional intake, improved hygiene and sanitary training and immunization would be crucial elements in this approach. Yet the philosophy of health care in Mexico concentrates upon individualized health care and treatment rather than on collective programmes to improve general living conditions. The Mexican Ministry of Health and Welfare (SSA) spends a disproportionate part of its budget on curative treatment (36%) and administration (36%) but only a miniscule proportion (12%) on preventive medicine, treatment and improvement of the environment, and training the population in the importance of hygiene (López Acuña 1980: 209, data for 1978). Moreover, as we observed in Chapter 1, the priority accorded to social welfare expenditure has declined since the early 1970s (Table 1.2). Although major advances have been recorded between 1970 and 1980 in servicing levels throughout the country, the absolute position of dwellings with inadequate sanitary and drinking water facilities is worse than ever before (Chapter 5).

The organization of health care in Mexico

Public health care and social security provision in Mexico have evolved over more than four decades and, paralleling expansion in other areas of the Mexican bureaucracy, present a pastiche of separate institutions, the individual fortunes of which have fluctuated with administrations. In Mexico, as elsewhere, there is a widely documented tendency for organizations to evolve as a response to pressure from the most powerful social groups. As Mesa Lago (1978: 6) argues for social security organizations (which often include health care institutions), 'Politically social security is seen as the result of the power that pressure groups have to extract concessions from the state or as a state instrument to neutralize and coopt such groups, avoid grave conflicts, and maintain the status quo and political stability.' But, in Mexico at least, coverage has also been extended to the not so powerful, and specifically to wider sections of the working population that include both blue- and white-collar workers. This has come about for various reasons. It is a result of political gestures initiated by past Executive to strengthen the popular ideology that the interests of the poor are being served. It has been used to win popular support for the government, while at other times it provides a means of compensating workers for declining opportunities and for the erosion of real wages.

In Mexico almost all social security institutions that have been established run their own medical service and it is difficult, therefore, to disaggregate data about expenditure and about broad policy changes that deal specifically with health matters. However, where possible I will attempt to focus solely upon health care. Also, given that the health and social security sector is a myriad of national and state institutions and programmes, I propose to analyse only the most important, measured in terms of their budgets and their coverage of the total population.

There are three broad sectors. First, there are public social security organizations, the largest of which is the IMSS (Instituto Mexicano de Seguro Social) founded in 1944. Next in size is the ISSSTE (Instituto de Seguridad y Servicios Sociales de los Trabajadores al Servicio del Estado) founded much later – in 1960 – for state employees. In addition there is a host of other medical and social security schemes often with their own hospitals and clinics. Amongst these the most important are for the military, railway, electricity, petroleum and sugar workers. However, given their relatively minor importance in terms of total number of affiliates I do not propose to consider them in any detail.

The second major level of health provision comes from the public–governmental sector and most important here is the SSA (Secretaría de Salubridad y Asistencia), a ministry which provides the main alternative source of health care for the bulk of the population not covered by any of the social security organizations. In addition there are organizations created to serve specific political administrative units such as the DDF's General Directorate of Medical Services which possesses a few clinics and hospitals but deals mostly with the distribution of free food and maintaining an adequate supply of blood for transfusions. Periodically, also, additional Federal agencies are created by the Executive to deal with specific needs or campaigns and are usually headed by the president's wife. Examples are the INPI (Instituto Nacional de la Protección de la Infancía), IMAN (Instituto Mexicano de Asistencia a la Niñez), and the DIF (Desarrollo Integral de la Familia), all of which are primarily concerned with children's welfare. Again these will be analysed only in so far as they shed light on particular points raised in my review.

Finally, the third sector comprises private medicine. This includes both a private health care system as well as private charitable institutions such as the Red Cross and the Green Cross. Although the latter are extremely limited in number and in the range of services that they offer, they represent an important 'bottom line' of health care provision. But the importance of a private health service in Mexico should not be underestimated. While the proportion of the total population covered by social security has risen from 22% in 1967 to almost 40% in 1980, this leaves the majority dependent upon the public–government and the private sector. Nor is private medicine only a preserve of the rich. As we shall observe later the poor make extensive use of the private sector for 'lightweight' consultations, and they may also receive private treatment paid for by their employer – a feature of patronage that remains widespread throughout Mexico.

Table 6.1 Health care facilities provided by different sectors and their per capita expenditure, 1972–83.

		Population to be attended (millions)	Doctors (000)	Hospital beds (000)	Nurses (all levels) (000)	Per capita expenditure (1978 pesos)
	SSA	39.5	0.25	0.64	nd	180
1972	IMSS	11.6	1.20	1.77	1.81	2866
	ISSSTE	1.8	2.30	1.57	2.39	3784
	SSA	40.8	0.45	0.86	nd	305
1978	IMSS	19.8	1.07	1.83	1.73	2587
	ISSSTE	5.0	1.26	0.95	1.36	4901
	SSA	51.42	0.32	0.69	nd	169[a]
1983	IMSS[a]	27.0	1.27	1.58	1.75	1829[a]
	ISSSTE[a]	5.8	1.82	0.98	2.30	3002[a]

Note
[a]   Preliminary figure.
Sources
Jóse López Portillo, *VI Informe, anexo 1* 1982, 658. IMSS *Memoria*, 1980: 37. De la Madrid, *Primer Informe del gobierno, Sector salud y seguridad social* 1983, various tables. *Segundo Informe del gobierno, anexo política económica* 1984, 697.

In the following sections no attempt is made to dissect the nature of provision through the private sector, though its importance should not be forgotten. Rather the concern is to identify the changing nature of coverage provided by the principal social security and government systems and to examine how each is financed. The changing commitment of past and present governments to health care provision is measured through an examination of the allocation of resources to each organization. Finally I look at various aspects of policy: its formulation, principal features and relative effectiveness.

Health care: who does what?
Since the late 1960s each of the three major public institutions has attempted to expand their coverage and to identify a clear responsibility for a particular section of the population. In the case of the ISSSTE there is little or no ambiguity about membership. ISSSTE covers all federal employees and offers the most extensive and generous health and social security package. Affiliation increased fivefold between 1966 and 1976, mirroring the expansion of the state bureaucracy during that period. Expansion was particularly rapid during the early 1970s although resources per capita have scarcely risen at all (Table 6.1). Almost all of its affiliates are urban and, as we can observe from Table 6.2, a high proportion live in the Metropolitan Area. Although a large part of its operations relates to welfare, pensions and mortgage loans, in absolute terms it still spends more on health care than the SSA (López Acuña 1980: 210).

Table 6.2 Population attended by social security organizations and by private and government sectors.

	Metropolitan Area[a]		Nation[b]	
	%	000s	%	000s
social security				
IMSS	43.0	4 935.8	29.9	20 000[c]
ISSSTE	15.5	1 772.1	7.2	4 800
others	7.2	828.0	2.2	1 500
government				
SSA and DDF	17.9	2 045.9	15.6	10 500
private sector	16.5	1 884.0	14.9	10 000
unattended	0.0	0.0	30.1	20 100
Total	100.1	11 465.8	100.0	66 900

Sources
[a] DDF, *Plan Director*, Ch. 7, based upon data provided by SSA. Data are for 1976.
[b] López Acuña (1980: 108), based on data from Jóse López Portillo, *II Informe*. Data are for 1978.
[c] Pre-IMSS–COPLAMAR programme (see Table 6.1 for more recent figures).

In contrast to this lack of ambiguity about coverage, access to the IMSS and to the SSA is much more likely to overlap largely because IMSS's prodigious resources have gradually been extended to 'marginal' or strictly 'non-labour' groups which ought, theoretically, to be served by the SSA. After its creation in 1944 the IMSS grew rapidly between 1955 and 1964, and since then it has grown steadily with one or two notable leaps in its membership where legislation such as the Social Solidarity Programme (1974) and the IMSS–COPLAMAR agreement (1979) have extended coverage to previously isolated groups. Nationally it is the dominant sector, providing coverage for almost 30% of the total population in 1978 and an even higher proportion of workers in the Metropolitan Area (Table 6.2). Traditionally just over one-half of the total IMSS budget is directed towards health care, though this rose in 1977 to around 65% (López Acuña 1980: 190, 210).

At the outset there should have been no ambiguity about accessibility to IMSS as it was specifically designed for urban salaried workers and, from 1954, for agricultural salaried workers as well. Yet in 1973, and in subsequent major additions, coverage has been made possible to all people in employment although they are accorded an inferior membership status. 'Obligatory' coverage is the most comprehensive, providing for all those in a worker–employer relationship. Theoretically this should include all domestic workers, agricultural wage earners and *ejidatarios* but in practice many are excluded. More recently 'voluntary' coverage has been introduced under the Social Solidarity Programme which makes provision for self-employed 'informal' sector workers to affiliate to IMSS, though the level of benefits is not as comprehensive and is limited to non–specialist medical treatment and exclude maternity care. In view of these limitations it is scarcely surprising that relatively few people have joined. Neither do rural workers receive the same level of benefits as those in urban areas. They receive full medical and maternity care but no invalidity pensions, sickness benefit nor special treatment for accidents incurred at work. Despite attempts to extend coverage to rural areas membership of IMSS remains overwhelmingly urban – 91% in 1983 (De la Madrid 1984 *Segundo Informe, anexo sector salud*).

The result of the expansion of IMSS coverage has been to create an overlap with medical attention provided by the SSA. Nevertheless, the government sector still retains its traditional role of providing for the majority of the national population who do not enjoy social security coverage or private medical insurance. In absolute terms the responsibilities of the SSA have grown (Table 6.1). In 1983 the Minister of Health and Welfare stated that in rural areas alone between 15 and 20 million people were without any access to health care (*Excélsior*, 17 April 1983). The problem that the government sector faces is not so much one of defining its target population nor one of preserving its institutional integrity, but rather that of totally inadequate resources. Of the three institutions it is easily the worst endowed. Yet for the poor it represents a crucially important system. Estimates vary, but it seems likely that for between 18% and 20% of the population of the Metropolitan Area, the SSA system represents the only alternative to private medicine (Table 6.2). Almost three-quarters of this number are estimated to live within the Federal District, and the remainder in surrounding municipalities (DDF 1976 *Plan Director*, chapter 7).

The rise in numbers covered by each of these institutions has important implications for the manpower and health care resources that each is able to offer, particularly in the light of the earlier finding that in terms of real annual expenditure the social development sector has lost influence during the last decade (Ch. 1). Table 6.1 shows the sharp deterioration in the level of staffing and facilities offered by ISSSTE due in large part to a major increase of affiliates between 1973 and 1978. Per capita ratios of doctors, beds and nurses declined dramatically and its previous high position was eroded relative to IMSS which managed to maintain its earlier levels despite an increased membership. However, in neither case does the level of service drop to anything near the paucity of resources demonstrated by the SSA throughout the period. In the early 1980s per capita facilities enjoyed by the social security sector were vastly superior to those of the public–government sector.

Method of financing and institutional autonomy
In Chapter 1 we saw how the total share of resources allocated to the social development sector declined relative to other sectors of federal expenditure. Moreover, the proportion spent by the health and social security organizations has declined from 56% in the early 1970s to around one-half at the end of the

decade (Table 6.3). Much of this decline is the result of the IMSS losing part of its total share. Both ISSSTE and SSA have retained theirs throughout the period. Yet despite the reduction in the proportion of total government resources dedicated to health care, the sector has managed to maintain itself. In real terms gross expenditure has more than doubled over the decade 1972–82 (Table 6.3). In per capita terms the picture is less rosy, and while each institution has managed to sustain its earlier level of funding all three have suffered cuts in 1983 (Table 6.1). Therefore I cannot be as condemnatory as López Acuña (1980: 199) who bemoans that per capita expenditure in overall health care had not even been doubled. Nevertheless, it does suggest that government priority for health and social security throughout this period has been one of maintenance rather than one of development and expansion.

All three agencies are dependent to some extent on federal government resources and although the proportion received fluctuates slightly from year to year it has remained at around the same level throughout. There has been no sharp withdrawal nor infusion of state funds that would drastically alter the nature of the service provided. Government financial support for the IMSS stands at around 10% while for ISSSTE it is between 33% and 44%. It is assumed that practically all of SSA's budget comes from the government, although López Acuña (1980: 187) points out that its funding actually derives

Table 6.3 Total expenditure of different health care organizations expressed in constant (1978) peso (millions) and as a percentage of total expenditure on 'social development'.

	IMSS		ISSSTE		SSA		Total	
	Constant pesos	Percentage of social development sector[a]	Constant pesos	Percentage of social development sector[a]	Constant pesos	Percentage of social development sector[a]	Constant pesos	Percentage of social development sector[a]
1972	33 243	37	10 412	12	7 123	8	50 778	56
1974	42 121	35	19 294	16	7 863	7	69 274	58
1976	49 165	27	24 461	13	9 450	5	83 076	45
1978	51 230	29	24 503	14	12 460	7	88 193	50
1980	64 577	31	30 009	14	13 145	6	107 731	52
1982	73 208	29	20 558	8	13 193	5	106 959	42
1983[b]	54 828	32	17 321	10	8 690	5	80 839	47

Notes
[a] Figures may be slightly inaccurate due to rounding.
[b] Provisional figure.
Sources
Data for IMSS and ISSSTE are drawn from López Portillo, *VI Informe, Anexo 1*. SSA data are from the same source, *Anexo histórico*: 19–24. Data for 1981–3 are drawn from De la Madrid, *Segundo Informe del gobierno, Sector salud y seguridad social*, various tables.

from a mosaic of sources that includes federal, state and municipal contributions; private companies; the national lottery; its own investments, and sundry
charges to the sick. IMSS is funded on a tripartite basis comprising government,
employers and employees. Its real income cannot be substantially increased
without renegotiating a higher proportional levy from either employers or from
labour. During periods of restraint on wage increases such as that experienced
during the first year of De la Madrid's administration it is likely that there will
be an erosion of institutional funds – unless, of course, government intervenes
to make good the loss.

Health policies over three administrations
Throughout the three administrations there has been no fundamental shift in the
philosophy that underpins health care in Mexico, which continues to be
primarily curative. Although as we observed in Chapter 5 a significant effort has
been made to improve environmental living conditions, this has not formed an
integral part of a preventive health care policy. In Mexico, as elsewhere, the
medical profession is relatively conservative and is loath to give up or to change
radically the existing structure. Nonetheless, within the framework of a
curative philosophy important shifts have occurred. These have been influenced
fundamentally by two factors: first, the impact of different political administrations and personalities, specifically the initiatives stimulated by the Executive;
and secondly, the level of resources allocated to health care. Only when cash
is available can policy makers espouse large and grandiose plans. When cash is
severely restricted then the arguments for self-help and for community
medicine are dusted off and, to mix metaphors, are displayed in new bottles.

During the early 1970s under Echeverría the emphasis lay firmly on
developing large-scale, high technology hospitals and medical centres which
López Acuña (1980: 182) describes as 'white elephants which, voraciously,
consume scarce resources allocated to health care in Mexico'. In Mexico City the
IMSS in particular has tended to concentrate its resources in the running of the
huge medical centres such as Centro Médico and La Raza, as well as other large
hospitals. Additionally the emphasis upon gynaecology during the early 1970s
reflected the specialist interests of the director of the period. During Echeverría's
presidency the big-spending medical sectors appeared to be eager to emulate
Western technological systems of curative medicine. However, as we have seen
in previous chapters, Echeverría also espoused more 'populist' programmes
which had potentially wide-reaching implications for improving community
health care but which ended up as little more than rhetorical gestures. For
example, the Executive encouraged the activities of institutions such as INPI
and IMAN and created general purpose community development agencies such
as INDECO. The actions of many of these agencies were usually rather
lightweight, consisting of the distribution of breakfasts, education about
nutrition, rehabilitation and education of polio victims, health and immunization campaigns and so on. These institutions had the advantage of being

relatively cheap, yet they were sufficiently flexible to respond to specific crises, as well as adding to the general ideology that significant action was being undertaken on behalf of the underprivileged. We have already seen in previous chapters parallel examples in the housing, servicing and land regularization fields.

Another example is the extension of limited coverage to 'informal' sector workers through the Social Solidarity Programme, although the health care provided was very superficial. Official statistics estimate that some 740 000 individual consultations took place in 1975 and increased to an annual figure of around 1.5 million between 1975 and 1981 (López Portillo *VI Informe, anexo 1* 1982: 679–80). However, it seems likely that these figures are somewhat inflated.

For the SSA, despite its low level of resources and brief to treat the bulk of the nation's poor, many of whom live in isolated rural communities, the focus during this period was also upon the more expensive kinds of medical attention. In addition there was intense political pressure exerted upon the Comisión Constructora, which until 1977 was an important subdepartment of SSA responsible for the planning and construction of hospital facilities. Our interviews with agency personnel led me to believe that some 30–40% of decisions taken by the Commission were political in nature (see also López Acuña 1980: 221). However, even where patronage was being extended to state governors, the requests for medical facilities had to be justifiable at least to some extent on technical grounds. When Echeverría intervened on behalf of the future governor of Chiapas to locate a 200-bed psychiatric hospital in the State capital of Tuxtla Gutiérrez, it was turned down for technical reasons.

A National Health Plan did emerge in 1974 following a Pan-American Conference on health. Many of the proposals contained in the plan were perfectly sensible and urgently required: a network of hospitals; the widening of health care to rural areas using small health centres; the wider distribution of medical and paramedical personnel to neglected areas; a nutrition programme and so on. But adequate resources were never allocated for their implementation. López Acuña (1980: 222) condemns the Plan as 'propagandist and doctrinaire and one of the worst instances of official rhetoric'. He goes on to say that 'in reality the aims put forward in the plan contained a fundamental flaw which made it purely demagogic and voluntaristic in-so-far as the wide-ranging proposals were never converted into realistic norms and strategies' (*ibid.*: 222). Although the Plan was designed to be implemented in two stages ending in 1982 it was immediately scrapped in 1977 for lack of resources and for being unrealistic in its aims.

Significant changes in policy date from the beginning of López Portillo's government. Health agencies attempted some reorganization of the structure of medical care that made more vigorous emphasis upon the need for local communities to have greater access to general services, and to 'soft-pedal' on costly investment programmes in the fields of intensive care and specialist treatment. This reorganization was induced by the rather more downbeat style of the new president and by his initiatives to streamline the public bureaucracy and to make it more efficient. A Health Sector Cabinet was created in an attempt to integrate those institutions with a major concern in health matters. The change of policy also related to the lack of resources during the austerity period between 1977 and 1979 and I have already described how in terms of allocating resources to the SSA López Portillo was not much more forthcoming than his predecessor.

In the Metropolitan Area the IMSS has attempted to respond to earlier criticism that it has tended to neglect general medical care in favour of highly specialized treatment, and has reorganized its health care system. General medical care became the hallmark of policy between 1977 and 1982 and a new hierarchy of treatment was established. This consisted of medical centres and specialist hospitals at the top level, which remained much as before but with no proposals for expansion. Next, zonal general hospitals (ZGH) were created with three sizes depending upon the number of specializations practised within them; and finally, family medical units were established comprising surgeries to provide out-patient treatment, but closely linked to the ZGHs. It is difficult to say whether this simply represents a minimal shuffling of the existing structure or a genuine change. Clearly, family medical units were a new feature but it is unclear how extensive they became. Certainly they do not feature in my spatial analysis of separate institutions (below). Where they were established in the Metropolitan Area it seems likely that they were created as units within existing facilities.

In laying down priority guidelines for the SSA, López Portillo identified 2 out of the 57 programmes contained within Echeverría's National Health Plan. These were a programme of community health centres and another for family planning. The first resulted in the formation of PEC (a programme for extending health service care to rural and suburban environments) in 1977, which employed auxiliaries to extend health care to 13 666 localities. Auxiliary staff were local inhabitants who were paid a small retainer by SSA, given minimal training, and provided with briefcases containing some basic medical items and an instruction manual, and then sent back to their communities as undertrained, 'barefoot' doctors (López Acuña 1980: 227). Whatever the other failings of this programme it also overlapped with a rural community programme developed by a different group within the same ministry. This involved the training of different community auxiliaries in family planning, co-ordinated by a specialist nurse. The obvious overlap prompted the SSA later to combine both into a programme of rural health.

In the Metropolitan Area similar attempts were made by SSA to develop education about health problems and to carry out preventive work within the *delegaciones*. This comprised a hierarchy: main health centre, health centre, community health centre. Meanwhile, a separate department was created to deal with 'marginal' areas. It identified that some 700 local health centres were required, yet by 1979 only 59 were said to have been established. Because funds were scarce, the costs of these centres were to be covered by the *delegaciones* and by residents, with only minor financial assistance from the SSA. These programmes suggest that the administration's heart was in the right place, but the perennial problem of inadequate funding combined with poor administration and unnecessary overlap meant that the achievements were extremely limited.

Partly because the SSA was proving so inadequate and had failed to extend health care to rural areas, an agreement was reached between IMSS and a then recently created, decentralized agency called COPLAMAR which was responsible for 'marginal' and 'deprived' groups. This agreement, signed in 1979, aimed to construct 2000 rural and urban medical units and 52 rural clinics in arid, marginal and indigenous zones. The programme was to develop initially around an existing IMSS stock of 310 medical units and 30 clinics which had been partly developed under the largely defunct Social Solidarity Programme, while in the subsequent two years a further 1690 units and 10 hospital/clinics were to be built. Those people who benefited and received medical attention as a result would not have to pay, but they were expected to give up some of their labour as a contribution to the scheme. Federal funds were to be provided, but in 1979 these amounted to only 2661 million pesos (López Acuña 1980: 233).

Clearly this agreement should have been signed with the SSA and not with IMSS. Between 1979 and 1981 the number of individual consultations provided under the scheme is stated to have risen from 600 000 to over 4.5 million, with some 13.3 million people enjoying access to its services (López Portillo *VI Informe, anexo histórico* 1982: 682–3). In the event, President De la Madrid closed COPLAMAR in 1983.

The economic crisis since 1982 has also affected the nature of health care policies. The decline in resources in real terms has meant that most actions to date have sought to achieve greater administrative efficiency against the backcloth of presidential initiatives for a decentralization of public administration. Paper-shuffling reorganizations cost little. A Federal Health Law was passed in 1984 (*Diario Oficial*, 7 January 1984) to establish a National Health System. The SSA continues to be responsible for the general co-ordination of health and social welfare throughout the country and this measure is aimed at achieving far greater intra- and inter-sector co-ordination (Soberon & Narro 1984). Since 1983 there has been considerable decentralization of health care services both of the SSA as well as of facilities created under the IMSS–COPLAMAR Social Solidarity Programme. In both cases individual states take over responsibility for health care and welfare programmes. Another feature of policy induced by the economic crisis is an emphasis upon community participation both in health care and also in local preventive and educational campaigns. The irony is that only a lack of resources has induced some shift away from purely curative philosophies of health care.

The Metropolitan Area: a privileged minority

We have seen that there are marked differences in the standard of service offered by the two major social security organizations compared with that of the government sector. As López Acuña notes (1980: 113), over 50% of doctors, general nurses, and administrative and auxiliary staff are concentrated in the social security institutions while the government welfare agencies, which have to cope with a much larger total population, enjoy only 20% of the same resources.

Some concentration of resources in the capital city is both justifiable and desirable. It is sensible to locate centres of specialist surgery in the largest cities which offer relatively easy access to a large hinterland population, themselves constitute a large demand, and have the necessary support services and facilities. Yet in 1978 almost one-third of the population were, in effect, unserved by any formal health care system. This compares unfavourably with conditions in the Metropolitan Area where everyone has access to one system or another (Table 6.2). To this extent those living in Mexico City might be called privileged. Despite the significant extension of coverage achieved by the IMSS–COPLAMAR agreement, between 15 and 20 million Mexicans are without access to health care services, most of them in rural areas (SSA in *Excélsior*, 17 April 1983). The same source indicated that 30% of the population sought medical assistance through the private sector, a point to which we shall return later.

Resources are highly unequally distributed within the nation. The poorest rural states such as Oaxaca and Chiapas in the south have a very low number of doctors and beds while the Federal District is approximately three times better off than the national average. Using certain specified 'norms' calculations projected to 1982 of regional deficits of doctors, nurses and hospital beds showed major deficiencies in most regions (Mexico COPLAMAR 1982: 339–41). In contrast the Central Valley of Mexico comprising the Federal District and the State of Mexico has an excess of doctors and nurses though it, too, has insufficient hospital beds. The same source estimates that this area has almost 50% more doctors than are required. In 1981 a total of 39% of the federal public investment in health and social security went to the Federal District, as did almost one-half of the investment budget for public health and welfare. After the central zone, the North, Pacific North, West and South-east Peninsular are the best endowed. The remaining seven regions are extremely deficient in all respects.

There is, of course, another consideration and that is the type of service offered. If many of the doctors and nurses who work in Mexico City are primarily engaged in specialist medicine or in private practice, then for the bulk of the city population who do not make use of it or who cannot afford private medicine the 'relative advantage' of Mexico City is lessened. Certainly a large proportion of doctors working in Mexico City's health institutions are contracted as 'specialists' – something like 30% according to one source. Indeed the large majority of graduate doctors are specialists and only a few go into what we would understand as general practice (López Acuña 1980: 116). It is also true that many work in private practice either exclusively or part-time with a post in the public sector. Although the data are imprecise, it appears that only a minority work solely in the public sector. Therefore given that much of the specialist and private medicine practised in Mexico is located in the capital city, the actual relative advantage enjoyed by the bulk of the population is perhaps rather less than might appear at first sight. Nevertheless, for people in Mexico City access to health care is far greater than for a rural or urban provincial counterpart, particularly if he or she happens to live somewhere in Chiapas or Oaxaca, which stand out as the most impoverished states.

Access to adequate health care facilities is not simply a question of their availability or that they be of the right kind: it is also a matter of their being located at accessible points throughout the city. Large, intensive-care specialist hospitals form an integral part of any hierarchy of provision and can normally be expected to be located near the centre of the city or at a nodal point within the city's transport network. More important, however, is the need to achieve a balance and to ensure an adequate distribution of general treatment facilities (Eyles & Woods 1983: 131). In Mexico City a broad hierarchy exists comprising integrated medical centres, general hospitals, clinics and health centres. This is complemented by specialist hospitals and institutes. The latter together with the multifaceted medical centres provide a service for the national and regional population. Given the enormous costs of establishing and maintaining these institutions it is reasonable to locate them in the largest urban centres. However, one may question the desirability of duplicating all levels of the hierarchy for

Table 6.4 Social security coverage and source of treatment by settlement, 1979 (percentages).

	Isidro Fabela	El Sol	Santo Domingo los Reyes	Jardines de Tepeyac	Liberales	Chalma Guadalupe	Total
households with no social security coverage	26	45	41	44	20	27	35
cases where person treated had social security	83	49	51	54	65	62	60
sector in which treated							
charity/government	7	16	24	31	18	2	17
private treatment	30	63	37	33	18	36	38
social security	63	21	39	36	64	61	45
total number of households	81	68	75	59	22	44	349

Source
PIHLU settlement survey, 1979.

Table 6.5 Type and institutional source of treatment for residents in irregular settlements.

Type of treatment	Percentage	Number
consultations		
in a hospital	2.3	8
by a private doctor	26.9	94
in a health centre (SSA)	6.6	23
in a private clinic	2.3	8
in a social security clinic	27.8	97
with a 'quack'	0.6	2
with a nurse	1.7	6
total consultations	68.2	238
hospitalization		
government or charity	7.7	27
private hospital	6.9	24
social security	16.9	59
total hospitalization	31.5	110

Source
PIHLU settlement survey, 1979.

each sector. IMSS, ISSE and SSA each have large medical centres in Mexico City, and in some cases more than one.

In this chapter I am not concerned to explain why that situation has come about; rather my wish is to analyse the effective coverage that exists throughout the Metropolitan Area. If we examine more closely the location of public health services in the city the glaring inadequacy of coverage becomes apparent. In 1965 when rapid suburbanization of low-income settlement had already been underway for two decades, there was minimal provision of health centres within easy reach of these poor districts. In the East, South-east and North-east there were virtually no public sector facilities. Most medical services were aligned in a horseshoe shape around Chapultepec Park with an especially large number situated around the city centre. In essence the older, established and richer parts of the city were well served.

Yet despite more than a doubling of population between 1965 and 1980, and the fact that most of the increase has been concentrated in the more suburban *delegaciones* and adjacent municipalities, the pattern established before 1965 has not altered appreciably (Fig. 6.1).[1] Although there has been some growth of new facilities in the periphery, they are widely scattered. Both ISSSTE and IMSS have done little more than consolidate their existing network, creating new medical centres and large hospitals but showing little real effort to decentralize coverage in the form of health centres and clinics to poor suburban districts. Granted, ISSSTE's unwillingness to shift is partly justifiable on the grounds that only a relatively small proportion of its affiliates live in the low-income

Table 6.6 Sector in which treatment was sought according to whether respondent had social security coverage (percentages).

Sector in which treated	All	Without social security	With social security
government and charity	17	32	7
private	39	62	25
social security	45	6	68
total	101	100	100
total number of respondents	(349)	(129)	(195)

Source
PIHLU settlement survey, 1979.

settlements. But the same is not true for IMSS: in the PIHLU survey no fewer than 65% of households interviewed were members of IMSS.

The SSA have made some attempt to increase access to their facilities and to shift the locus of services towards poorer areas. As we have seen, the government sector has primary responsibility for approximately one-fifth of the Metropolitan population. Between 1965 and 1971 the SSA initiated a reorganization of its facilities and closed several of its outlets downtown while opening others in the poorer districts of the Federal District. The DDF's Directorate of Medical Services also opened several clinics around this time. Throughout the 1970s the SSA continued to extend access to health care to peripheral low-income areas and from 1977 was joined by a marked expansion of the charity sector. Between them these two sectors have taken the major initiatives in extending health care facilities to poor districts of the city.

Health care for residents of irregular settlements

The 1979 household survey included various questions about family illnesses suffered during the preceding twelve months, the treatment received, and opinions relating to the quality of medical attention. These data are partial in the sense that they only give an indication of health patterns for low-income residents in the *colonias populares* of Mexico City at one particular time. However, they provide a basis for independent evaluation of the efficiency of the health care system, and several of the findings are interesting in the context of the preceding discussion.

Although there was undoubtedly some under-reporting of minor or short-lived illnesses (such as colds or intestinal complaints), more than one-half of all households interviewed declared that at least one member of the immediate family had been ill during the previous twelve months. In the majority of cases the person specified was the wife (36%) or a child (42%). It often proved

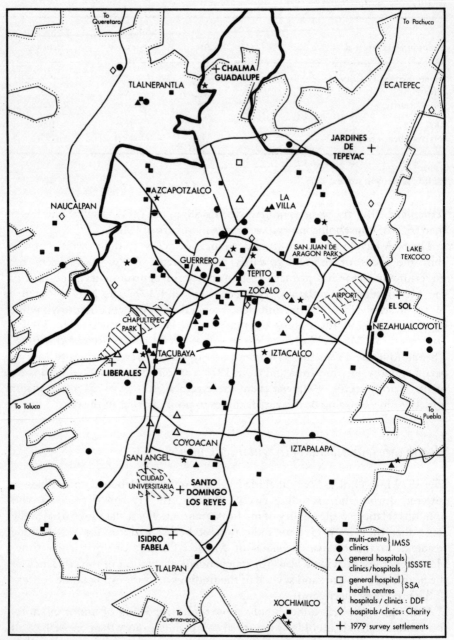

Figure 6.1 Locations of institutions providing medical treatment in 1982.

difficult to identify with any precision the true nature of the illness as many were 'minor' ailments that did not fit any easy categorization. In those cases where the illness was specified a significant number related to some sort of natal care or to treatment for influenza. Intestinal disorders also figured but were probably under-reported or form a large part of an 'unspecified' illness category.

The source of treatment received appears to relate to two considerations. The first is whether or not the individual was covered by any form of social security health care. Secondly, choice intervenes in that not everyone automatically used the cheapest system available to them. As we have already observed, an estimated 66% of the city population is covered by social security health care – broadly similar to the proportion of heads of household in our sample, most of whom belonged to IMSS. Specifically, 60% of those individuals for whom an illness was reported were covered by one of the social security organizations, though that coverage varied considerably between settlements (Table 6.4). Yet despite the fact that the majority had social security, and that even those not covered had recourse to the government sector, many respondents opted for private treatment, usually by consulting a doctor at his surgery (Table 6.5). Indeed, almost two-fifths of all treatment was provided by the private sector (Table 6.6). It appears that the poor often trade-off the use of public sector facilities in favour of the more conveniently located private service. This is especially likely where the sickness is relatively minor and does not require intensive care or hospitalization. For the latter, and for treatments that are likely to prove expensive, the official and social security sectors are used almost exclusively. By and large people can afford a one-off payment to a local doctor; but they cannot contemplate the high costs of hospitalization or of sustained private treatment. This finding applies both to social security affiliates and to those not covered, although not equally. Those with social security are more likely to use that service but one-quarter of affiliates went 'private', compared with 62% of those without cover whose only alternative was the official or charity systems (Table 6.6).

Two explanations may be advanced for the extensive use of private medicine by the poor. First, it may indicate dissatisfaction with the public sector brought about by earlier unsatisfactory treatment, long waits or because people feel culturally alienated from using modern medicine. Yet none of these reasons appears likely given that practically everyone (over 80%) expressed satisfaction with the treatment received regardless of the sector that provided it. This does not necessarily mean that the service offered is satisfactory: but simply that low-income residents expressed few complaints.

A second explanation relates to accessibility. I have shown that there is a marked discrepancy between the location of public health facilities and low-income housing areas. Invariably the latter are poorly served. Most people, therefore, face a long journey on public transport or taxi to a government or social security clinic and, understandably, prefer to visit the local doctor, often in the same settlement. In most of the survey settlements the majority sought private treatment in the immediate vicinity of their homes. Alternatively, or in cases where specialist treatment was required, they went to the nearest appropriate institution (Fig. 6.2). These are indicated by the thicker -line flows on Figure 6.2, and one can see that this often means a journey of considerable distance, especially in the most peripheral settlements such as Jardines de Tepeyac and Isidro Fabela. The average (crow-flight) round-trip distance to the place of treatment in these two settlements was 12.5 and 10 kilometres respectively. Even residents in the better served settlements such as Chalma Guadalupe and Santa Domingo los Reyes had to travel an average of 6 kilometres. Paradoxically, El Sol, which is one of most poorly served of all, appears to be not so badly off (8 kilometres), but this is because most residents have no alternative but to use the private *local* facilities, thereby reducing the settlement average travel distance recorded (see Fig. 6.2).[2]

As we have seen elsewhere in this study the frequent failure of the state to provide an adequate service means that many of the poor are obliged to make their own arrangements and to provide for themselves. For the sake of convenience a substantial minority use private facilities and in the event of a relatively minor ailment most go to a nearby doctor. Although private consultations are relatively inexpensive in these districts, it is a paradox that the poor should make extensive use of this sector given that a comprehensive public system is supposed to exist. It emphasizes the need for a wider distribution of local health centres in peripheral areas of the city. In particular the SSA should direct greater investment towards low-cost community health care facilities given that it is the population dependent upon that sector which uses private doctors with greatest frequency.

Community involvement in the provision of health care facilities
In several areas of public intervention community mobilization is a critical ingredient determining the allocation and spatial distribution of resources (Ch. 5). Indeed, as we saw in the case of the SSA's 'marginal areas' project for the Federal District, community labour and participation were a prerequisite to reduce the overall cost of public works. However, none of the survey settlements appears to have benefited from that scheme. Overall, it is rare for communities to mobilize around a health care issue. In Chapter 5 we observed that certain services such as land regularization, water and electricity provision appear to promote greater community involvement and mobilization than others. Health care does not attract community participation (Table 5.2). Very few households mentioned participating in lobbying the government, or any other activity, in pursuit of improved local health care facilities. In one settlement (Isidro Fabela), a purpose-built community centre was constructed by an agency called Servicios Metropolitanas and included a surgery. Yet it never functioned because neither *colonia* residents nor officialdom was really interested in it. Few respondents mentioned the desirability of improved health care facilities as a local priority issue.

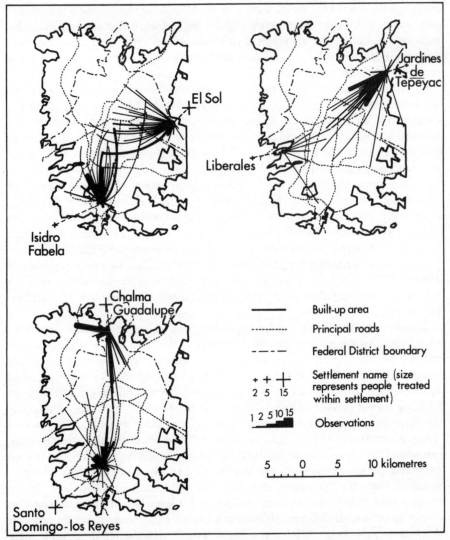

Figure 6.2 Places of medical treatment for residents of six irregular settlements in Mexico City.

There are several structural and ideological reasons for this. First, unlike water, electricity, drainage and perhaps regularization, which are 'collectively consumed' (i.e. consistently required by the large majority of the community), health and education are 'consumed' individually and ephemerally. Those who have children of school age send them to school; and demands vary according to the presence or absence of children and according to their ages. Not everyone has an interest in school provision. The same argument applies to health: not everyone has a need for medical treatment. Most tend to trust their luck and to hope that a member of their family will not fall seriously ill. If they do, then that *individual* seeks appropriate medical attention. Hence settlement leaders identify only those services which they know are likely to evince widespread support as the principal focus of mobilization.

However, this does not explain why, once collectively needed services are acquired, people do not turn their attention to health care. In part this is explained by a second reason. In Mexico the smallest institutional level of health care service commonly found is that of a clinic or health centre. Usually they are designed to serve several settlements. Therefore, if pressure is to be applied to persuade government to provide a facility, it must be co-ordinated between various communities. Several factors militate against this happening. Few settlements are at the same level of 'integration' in terms of service provision. Even in adjacent communities the local leadership will generate a different rank order of priorities for future actions. Moreover, the vertical nature of relations between individual settlements and individual politicians and agencies in Mexico acts, quite deliberately, against communities working together in unison. From a leader's point of view, mobilization around a health care issue which requires collaboration with neighbouring communities is usually a non-starter.

Thirdly, one should not underemphasize the ideological role that a stratified social security system exercises in preventing the emergence of social action around health care issues. In irregular settlements in Mexico some of the population have full IMSS coverage; others have partial IMSS coverage; and a few belong to ISSSTE. Everyone else knows that should they fall ill then the SSA, or a local private doctor, will provide appropriate attention. Once again the interests of community members are split various ways from the outset. There is not likely to be a single view about the necessity for improved facilities nor about the type of provision that should be sought. In addition, as we have observed, people do not perceive health care provision as a problem. Most are satisfied with the treatment that they receive. Although objective criteria suggest that health care in Mexico City is inadequate and unequal, the very existence of several different sources of treatment encourages satisfaction with the status quo. Those who want health care benefits offered through social security schemes know that the most feasible way to achieve it is by securing a job where it is provided automatically, and not by pressing the state to provide it to the whole population. The blame is perceived to rest with the individual for not having the right job, not with the state for failing to provide a universal service.

Neither are existing pressure groups which have won social security benefits for their members likely to press for changes that would make the system more equitable. They will continue to press only for improvements for their membership and fight to maintain their relative advantage over competing pressure groups. As in the past, any future significant change in the nature of health care provision for the majority will derive from governmental initiative and largesse, rather than as a result of organized trades union or settlement mobilization.

Conclusion

This chapter has reviewed policy for health care over three administrations. We have seen that while marked shifts in policy are detectable, ultimately they have had little effect. The philosophy remains firmly one of curative medicine and there has been no concerted attempt to improve preventive care in local communities through better water and sewerage provision, raised levels of nutrition, and general hygiene training. There has been some reduction in the priority accorded to investment in intensive care facilities in favour of the need to provide more general forms of health care to a large body of the population. But in Chapter 1 we observed that, although as a national priority the 'social development' sector which contains health care has been eroded in recent years, in absolute terms expenditure has grown: twofold in real prices since the early 1970s. Therefore we cannot conclude that the standard of care has declined, though it may have deteriorated in per capita terms.

Another problem encountered when reviewing policies has been the tendency for initiatives to be superficial. The majority of the population remain outside the various tiers of health care offered by the principal social security agencies which is, by and large, superior to that received through the SSA. Improvements are minor and have usually comprised attempts to extend coverage of the IMSS to populations that were previously uncovered. Although this is welcome, the coverage offered is minimal and inferior to that received by existing members of the same social security institution. This serves to create yet another tier within an already highly stratified system. Large infusions of extra resources are necessary if the SSA is ever to provide an adequate system of health care for the majority of the population. The shifts in policy observed over the three administrations are best explained in terms of the 'style' of each president, the degree of organized pressure from social security interest groups and the availability of resources for expenditure on health care.

Secondly, we have examined the structure of the health care system in Mexico. For a developing country the multiplicity of parallel and sometimes overlapping organizations with responsibilities for health care is both wasteful of resources and inefficient. There is a low level of linkage between the organizations and relatively little integration achieved by the SSA despite initiatives such as a 'health sector cabinet' and, more recently, the National Health System. Moreover the method of financing the different social security organizations is regressive (Mesa Lago 1978: 254). Contributions are a proportion of wages, so that although better-off groups pay greater sums, so do the rest of the tripartite of contributors, be they government or employer

(Midgley 1984). If the latter, contributions are usually generated from profits on goods so the consumer ends up paying. As a result those organizations which offer cover to better-paid workers and employees are most likely to build up their resources quickly. Clearly this multiplicity of structures is not an historical accident. It is a deliberate outcome of the political system and facilitates the manipulation of one sector or group of the population against another. It also makes the structure highly resistant to change. Few groups will wish to concede the advantage they hold.

This leads to my third general conclusion that the existing structure has important ideological functions for the state. Covertly the health and social security systems serve to co-opt the most powerful or organized groups in society. Thus federal workers are catered for through ISSSTE, and those in strategic industries enjoy their own health care facilities, as do the military. These conditions, together with wider benefits provided by each individual social security system, have evolved in response to pressure from these more powerful groups (Mesa Lago 1978). All along they have sought to maintain their relative advantage *vis-à-vis* other groups. IMSS offers the best medical service but its social security benefits are not as generous as others. The SSA, which caters for the majority of the population, is no more than a nominal health service. This situation would probably not persist if those people or communities without adequate coverage organized more effectively to make demands or displayed a propensity to protest. Currently the state can afford to offer the bare minimum. In addition it has created a range of one-off 'troubleshooting' institutions which appear to make concessions or provide relief where it is required. Ideologically too, the failure of the state to provide an adequate health care system for all of its population is not perceived as a failing of the state. Rather the individual is 'blamed' for not having the right sort of job that would provide access to good medical care and social security benefits. Conversely, those who enjoy coverage provided by IMSS know that 'outside' they would be reliant upon SSA. These perceived privileges or 'perks' help further to induce passivity among the workforce.

Notes

1 I am grateful to Mr Stephen Melligan for his assistance in compiling the data for Figure 6.1 and for the other comparative figures not displayed in the text. The Department of Geography at University College London kindly provided financial assistance towards their production.

2 At first sight these distances may appear not unreasonable. However, they are conservative estimates based upon crow-flight distances and make no allowances for inefficient transport networks and transport systems. They are also averages and include the low distances associated with intra-settlement treatment. Also, one should bear in mind that few people in London would expect to travel more than two kilometres to see their doctor and not a great deal further to a hospital casualty department.

7 Social welfare in Mexico: papering over the cracks?

I now return to the subtitle of this book. Most English readers will be familiar with the idiom 'papering over the cracks', describing attempts to cover up underlying defects. Home decorators, faced with a wall in which the plaster is 'dead' or badly cracked, know that the only permanent solution is to hack off the defective material and replaster. Only then can the surface be painted afresh. However, this requires extra expense and probably the assistance of an expert plasterer. Most of us take the easier short-term alternative which is to seal the wall as best we can, wallpaper over the cracks and, if desired, paint over the papered surface. The result is that we cover up the underlying structure and avoid confronting the inadequacies; we create an impression that all is well. Indeed, in the short term the result may be highly satisfactory – particularly if in the meantime we sell up and move elsewhere!

Past approaches to social welfare provision in Mexico have covered structural failings within Mexican society and aptly fit this metaphor. Policies adopted are invariably short-term palliatives in response to specific economic or social pressures, but they sustain a bright and industrious image of a state concerned with the welfare of its less economically advantaged groups. Although governments cannot sell up and move elsewhere, Mexico's *sexenio* system does create an in-built tendency to avoid long-term social welfare programmes. Instead, short-term policy modifications are adopted. Some benefits may accrue to the poor, but these are usually partial, superficial and unsustained.

The appropriateness of the metaphor is reviewed in the light of the following questions. First, what are the most significant 'cracks' in contemporary Mexico? Secondly, what role does social welfare provision play in covering over those cracks? Finally, have conditions for the poor deteriorated or improved, and what can they expect from the future in the absence of major structural change?

Most of the 'cracks' in Mexico's political economy are not new. Neither the orthodox development strategies adopted, nor windfalls from petroleum, significantly altered long-standing economic inequalities. Exploitation, low wages and poor living conditions in the countryside remain. Land reform, rural development schemes, and state intervention to support small-scale farming and the production of staple foodstuffs failed to reduce inequality in rural areas. This inequality has been supplemented by growing poverty in the cities. On balance, however, urban areas probably offer better life chances for the poor. It is the wealthy and middle classes who have benefited most from economic growth. In order to cope with conflicting pressures from different economic and social groups, the state exercises a 'relative autonomy' from the dominant classes and, in order to ensure their long-term survival, may sometimes take action against them.

Socially, too, the cracks of social unrest that appeared during the late 1960s, far from disappearing, have been brought back into sharp perspective by recent austerity measures. Employment opportunities are not being generated fast enough to accommodate the expanding workforce. High levels of unemployment and underemployment since 1982 have affected both the poor and the middle classes. Wage rates are low, and the value of real wages has declined since 1982. The majority of the poor do not have access to basic essentials such as adequate housing, health care, services, or nourishing and varied diets. However, pressure for change is not uniform. Some regions are far worse off than others, and rural areas are invariably poorly endowed compared with cities. The poor, too, comprise a very heterogeneous group with widely differing demands. They include those who have managed to secure a foothold in the land and employment markets and who perceive themselves as having 'made good'; while others have fared less well. Also, younger age groups are finding it difficult to make the same gains as their parents.

Increasingly, therefore, the poor are thrown back upon their own resources. In the absence of a comprehensive 'welfare state' alternative survival strategies must be devised. Thus households attempt to ensure that they are not dependent upon the earnings of a single member but try to maximize the range of jobs held by different members. If one of them gets a job with social security then the whole family can enjoy medical coverage. Certain types of family structures offer greater security and enhanced opportunities for full employment of household members. The wider family provides support during sickness, bereavement, and financial difficulties.

Periodically social pressures boil over into conflict and protest. There is unrest in many rural areas, and the 1970s saw 'social movements' emerge in several Mexican cities, most notably in the north. However, the state has usually managed to contain these pressures through patron–clientelism, co-option and, if all else fails, repression.

Politically, the traditional patterns of control are breaking down. Gone are the old-style political bosses, and their place has been taken by a largely technocratic elite. Opposition groups and alternative political parties are beginning to flex their muscles: in particular the PAN has won notable successes in several regions. At the same time the ability of the PRI to fulfil its traditional responsibility of providing legitimacy and engendering social control is under intense strain. In a trade union environment traditionally characterized by corrupt and government-coopted leaders, a democratic movement is gaining strength and may be expected to extend its influence once the dominant but elderly leadership disappears. Inevitably the state will find it increasingly difficult to control the unions and ensure their passivity and allegiance. There are even cracks in the institution of the presidency. Both Echeverría and López Portillo were vilified at the end of their administrations.

Social welfare and social control

Against this backcloth, social welfare provision represents an important means of relieving pressure. Although the outcome for the poor has often been positive, there seems little doubt that the primary function of social welfare has been one of social control and appeasement. I do not believe that this is part of a conspiratorial design, nor the result of a 'guiding' Executive hand. Rather it is an inevitable outcome of the Mexican political process which seeks to make minor, carefully controlled adjustments in response to competing claims from different social groups. That the nature of this provision has changed significantly over the past two decades is a result of the failure of traditional forms of appeasement. The state has been obliged to seek new measures in order to guarantee stability. The greater efficiency observed within many sectors of the bureaucracy is a result of the growing importance of the *técnicos*, and the fact that the individualistic patron–client responses of yesteryear were simply not generating a sufficient flow of resources to appease the majority. Promises and rhetoric were no longer enough.

The bureaucracy itself offers considerable scope for political manipulation through a multiplicity of institutions with overlapping or competing responsibilities. This is clearly apparent in the case of the Mexico City planning bureaucracy, land regularization and health care. It is less pervasive among the major servicing and power agencies because of their importance to economic production and because they are often partly supported by external sources of funding which require that they be run in a more technical manner. While there have been significant attempts to streamline some areas of public administration, overlaps are commonplace and inter-sectoral rivalry remains intense. This provides a career structure within government and allows those in highest positions of power to play off one group against another, or to shift support behind certain groups as part of the balancing act of Mexican politics.

The poor are also subject to political manipulation. This book has shown how assistance in the form of services, land, and regularization does not come of right: it has to be fought for. Although community participation in petitioning is not all-embracing among households in irregular settlements, it is much higher in Mexico than in most other Latin American countries. This is because many elements of social welfare provision form part of the process of negotiation between government and low-income groups. The channels whereby resouces flow out to the poor are carefully circumscribed. The state has sought to create channels that will ensure the emergence of less hostile community leadership and, in some cases, do away with the need for leaders altogether. Direct negotiations between government agency and individual *colono* have become an important feature of local interaction since the middle to late 1970s. But not all services must be competed for: some dimensions of social welfare such as health and education appear to be provided 'as of right'. They are the exceptions that prove the rule. The highly stratified nature of their supply (in the case of health care) and the marked regional and rural to urban variation in coverage (health and education) serve to divide the poor into differentially served, competing groups.

Ideologically, too, social welfare provision helps sustain existing economic relations. A multifaceted system of provision gives the impression of a state concerned and active on behalf of the poor. Conservativism, non-militancy and individual dependency are encouraged through various means. First, regional variations in the distribution of social welfare benefits act to encourage complacency and passivity in those areas with preferential access to resources, and to divert demand making towards other issues. For example, compared with the rest of the populace those in the Federal District are a privileged minority. Servicing levels and housing provision are much better than elsewhere. Those migrants who have moved from the provinces are likely to be satisfied that their housing and welfare is a considerable improvement over what they might otherwise have enjoyed. In a similar vein we have noted that the most powerful groups are best served in social security and health care benefits. They are unwilling to give up this advantage and seek to maintain differentials *vis-à-vis* other groups.

Secondly, among low-income groups the highly stratified nature of social welfare provision acts to *sustain* existing divisions. The various tiers of social security provision, for example, divide not only those who are covered from those who are not, but also draw a careful distinction between the levels of privilege that various groups enjoy. Even the extension of social security coverage by IMSS to some marginal groups, *campesinos* and self-employed workers, which ought to have had a homogenizing effect, has led to the creation of several new tiers of coverage within that single organization.

Similar differences emerge from housing and servicing policy. State actions to increase access to land for self-help housing, and to 'regularize' illegal titles, have not been accompanied by equivalent efforts on behalf of renters. Consequently there are growing conflicts of interest between low-income home owners in irregular settlements and those who rent. While renter households want services, they are cautious in case actions that lead to improvements and land regularization raise land values and drive up rents. The various modes of informal land acquisition create conflicts of interest in regularization. The existence of well-established settlements juxtaposed with fledgling communities may also lead to conflict between groups whose class position is ostensibly identical.

Thirdly, social welfare in Mexico has important ideological implications in that it helps to deflect the 'blame' for inadequate provision away from the state on to the individual. Those people excluded from social security construe this not as the fault of the state for failing to provide adequate cover for all, but as a result of the type of job that they hold. In a similar vein, a group of residents in Mexico City were informed that their settlement was ineligible for services since it fell outside the urban development plan, and were advised to 'participate' in the next revision of the *planes parciales* to ensure that they were subsequently included (*Unomásuno*, 8 April 83). The truth was that they were unlikely to receive services because insufficient resources had been made available or because they were too far from the primary network. The important point to recognize is that social welfare provision deflects mobilization away from class-based (horizontal) organization towards active (vertical) competition between many unequal social groups. Existing patterns of social stratification are, therefore, accentuated.

Improving or deteriorating levels of social welfare?

Although I have argued that the primary motive of social welfare provision is to stave off social unrest, it is important to form a conclusion about whether or not the overall outcome has been positive for the poor. Important changes have occurred and in many cases have resulted both in an extension of benefits and improvements in quality.

Expenditure on social welfare has increased significantly in real terms since the early 1970s. This has allowed considerable expansion of coverage. There has been an improvement in the way in which budgets are spent. Peso for peso, contemporary programmes of health care, servicing, housing and land regularization offer better value for money than ever they did under Echeverría. Responses today are more efficient, more 'low-tech' in approach, and more in tune with people's real needs. But as a priority social welfare has contracted. While overall public expenditure tripled in real terms between 1970 and 1982 that of social development only doubled. Policies have sought to sustain levels of social welfare provision rather than to use the benefits of economic growth to develop and improve conditions. Granted, *relative* levels of service deprivation improved considerably between the 1970 and 1980 census, as did the proportion with access to health care. Moreover, most people have been able to acquire land for self-help housing relatively cheaply. Combined, the costs of land, regularization and servicing were usually affordable to most low-income households. Yet in *absolute* terms the evidence suggests that poor living conditions and unequal access to adequate health care have increased. Growing state intervention to prevent informal land development for irregular settlement has reduced the scale of opportunities for land acquisition which are not being offset by the expansion of site and service programmes generated by FONHAPO and state housing agencies. Continuing rapid population increase means that there were more people without services in 1980 than a decade earlier. Similarly the absolute number of Mexicans dependent for health care upon the poorly endowed state sector (SSA) has increased, as has the number without any effective coverage whatsoever. We should also remember that where the extension of coverage has occurred this does not automatically imply that the service is provided. At certain times of the year there may be insufficient water to supply low-income settlements despite the existence of a domestic network. Similarly the poor make widespread use of private medicine because it is more convenient. The best that can be said for Mexico's social welfare programmes since 1970 is that they have run fast to stand still.

There has been an improvement in the way in which servicing agencies respond to the poor. The growing technocratization of the public bureaucracy has resulted in less complex and less particularistic procedures; corruption has been reduced and people's rights are more likely to be upheld. The decentralization of decision making has also assisted this process. But there has not been any increase in real participation by popular groups. Participation remains carefully controlled by government and, at best, comprises consultation or mobilization of labour for community development projects imposed from above. Nor has the nature of political groups changed. *Camarillas* remain and within them politicians still hold sway: the difference is that in addition to personal loyalty, leaders expect their followers and collaborators to deliver the goods in a way that was not always a prime consideration in the past.

Future prospects

It would be naive to imagine that social welfare policy in the future is likely to improve dramatically. Indeed recent trends suggest that while the Executive is aware of the need to take actions to ameliorate hardship brought about by the austerity programme, it is in fact reducing the proportion of expenditure on social development. If the government is not prepared to give this sector priority during times of acute necessity it is unlikely to respond any more positively once conditions improve. As in the past, social welfare programmes may be expected to expand in real terms when the economy is buoyant, but their expansion is likely to be less rapid than that of other sectors.

If significant progress is to be made in overcoming the existing high levels of social inequality in Mexico then several major changes will need to take place. First, greater priority will have to be accorded to social welfare expenditures. This is necessary to extend direct and indirect subsidies for housing and land development. Health care systems also need to be developed, both in quantity, and spatially focusing upon rural and marginal areas. The existing multiplicity of systems should be standardized into a single structure offering the same set of benefits to everyone. This would reduce much of the unnecessary duplication of resources: it would also lessen existing processes which accentuate stratification patterns. Greater expenditure is also required to begin to develop the range of benefits offered, particularly in the field of unemployment and sickness benefits. High levels of underemployment would make this a very costly charge on the Treasury, but it is important that the state begin to take greater direct responsibility for the social reproduction of the labour force, and to reduce its indirect reliance upon self-help, upon kinship networks and upon the endurance of continuing hardship.

A cultural shift is also desirable to break the existing system of patronage which permeates all levels of Mexican society. Patronage between employer and employee, between served and server, and between politicians and *colonos* encourages subservience and dependency. It is also undignified. A change in traditional practices of patronage will be very difficult to achieve. Patronage is often exercised unconsciously and, equally important, it is often consciously sought by the poor. A *patron*, even a domestic employer, may provide cash assistance in times of crisis, access to private doctors, cast-offs in clothing and so on. Change will only begin to occur if the state provides free access for all to social welfare benefits and strengthens and implements employment legislation.

Government patronage, too, would also need to be reduced, although as we have observed this seems to be happening already. Government officers today are more accountable than ever before, but individual influence and discretionary decision making on the part of powerholders remains entrenched. Genuine efforts to devolve responsibility are underway, but public participation tends to be nominal and consultative in nature.

Realistically, though, these changes are unlikely even in the long term, for they touch too closely upon the time-worn rules that underpin politics and decision making in Mexico. Social welfare provision in the future is likely to comprise more of the same. This book has examined past practices and suggests that neither the cynic nor the historian will find much cause for a change of heart, or for optimism. However, the perspectives of both are valuable in helping to identify the role of social welfare as a mechanism for papering over the cracks in Mexico.

Appendix   *Table describing the PIHLU survey settlements in Mexico City*

	Isidro Fabela	Santo Domingo los Reyes	El Sol	Liberales	Chalma Guadalupe	Jardines de Tepeyac
number of house lots	1 324[a]	7 500[b]	7 000[c]	640[d]	2 300[e]	1 780[f]
number of households[g]	3 494	12 200	11 270	755	4 270	4 330
average household size[h]	5.8	6.0	5.7	5.9	5.9	5.8
approximate total population	20 000	73 500	64 000	4 500	25 200	25 000
consolidation score[i]	25.4	21.2	23.3	17.9	20.7	23.8
density: average lot space per person (m²)[j]	29	25	33	25	34	52
% owner households[j]	63	81	70	82	74	66
% renter households[j]	15	4	13	13	10	19
% sharer households[j]	18	14	12	5	15	11
number of households interviewed	144	120	120	60	73	114

Notes
[a] Estimate based upon total plot count.
[b] FIDEURBE (1976:57). Based upon a total census for regularization.
[c] Cisneros (n.d.).
[d] Registration of lots and *socios*: leaders' archive.
[e] Estimate based upon our pre-survey listing of 14 (of 120) blocks.
[f] Estimates provided by the leader. The figure relates to the original subdivision. Most plots of 400m² have been further subdivided.
[g] Estimates based upon survey data of average number of households per plot multiplied by the total number of plots.
[h] Calculation derived from *barrio* survey data.
[i] An unweighted points score incorporating data about physical structure of the dwelling, services enjoyed, number of rooms and material possessions.
[j] Calculations derived from *barrio* survey data.

Source
PIHLU survey. Data collected as part of the ODA-sponsored research project 'Public intervention, housing and land use in Latin American cities, 1979–82. Data are for 1979.

References

Abrams, C. 1964. *Man's struggle for shelter in an urbanizing world*. Cambridge, Mass.: MIT Press.
Aguilar Martínez, G. 1984. *Política y planeación urbana en el Distrito Federal. Evolución y actualidad.* Paper presented to the Anglo-Mexican Symposium of Geographers in Mexico City, September. Mimeo.
Alonso, J. et al. 1980. *Lucha urbana y acumulación de capital*. Mexico DF: Ediciones de La Casa Chata.
Amato, P. W. 1969. Environmental quality and locational behaviour in a Latin American city. *Urban Affairs Quarterly* **5**, 83–101.
Amato, P. W. 1970. Elitism and settlement patterns in the Latin American city. *Journal of the American Institute of Planners* **36**, 96–105.
Andrews, F. M. and G. Phillips 1970. The squatters of Lima: who are they and what do they want? *Journal of Developing Areas* **4**, 211–24.
Angel, S. 1983a. Upgrading slum infrastructure: divergent objectives in search of a consensus. *Third World Planning Review* **5**, 5–22.
Angel, S. 1983b. Land tenure for the urban poor. In *Land for housing the poor*, S. Angel et al. (eds), 110–42. Singapore: Select Books.
Angel, S., R. Archer, S. Tanphiphat and E. Wegelin (eds) 1983. *Land for housing the poor*. Singapore: Select Books.
Araud, C. 1973. Direct and indirect employment effects of eight representative types of housing in Mexico. In *Studies on employment in the Mexican housing industry*, C. Araud, G. Boon, V. Urquidi and P. Strassman, 45–113. Paris: OECD.
Arias, P. and B. Roberts 1985. The city in permanent transition. In *Capital and labour in the urbanized world*, J. Walton (ed.), 149–75. London: Sage.
Azuela, A. 1983. La legislación del suelo urbano: auge o crisis? In Ediciones SIAP, *Relación campo-ciudad: la tierra, recurso estratégico para el desarrollo y la transformación social*, 514–31. Mexico DF: Ediciones SIAP.

Ball, N. 1984. Measuring Third World Security expenditure: a research note. *World Development* **12** (2), 157–64.
Barkin, D. and G. Esteva 1978. *Inflación y democracía: el case de México*. Mexico DF: Siglo XXI.
Baross, P. 1983. The articulation of land supply for popular settlements in Third World cities. In *Land for housing the poor*, S. Angel et al. (eds), 180–210. Singapore: Select Books.
Bazant, J. 1979. *Rentabilidad de la vivienda de bajos ingresos*. Mexico DF: Editorial Diana.
Bortz, J. 1983. La cuestión salarial actual. *Análisis Económico* **2**, 103–20. Mexico DF: UAM Azcapotzalco.
Brown, J. 1972. *Patterns of intra-urban settlement in Mexico City: an examination of the Turner theory*. Dissertation Series 40. Ithaca: Cornell University Latin American Studies Programme.
Burgess, R. 1982. Self-help housing advocacy: a curious form of radicalism. A critique of the work of John F. C. Turner. In *Self-help housing: a critique*, P. Ward (ed.), 55–97. London: Mansell.
Burgess, R. 1985. The limits of state self-help housing programmes. *Development and Change* **16**, 271–312.
Burns, L. and D. Shroup 1981. Effect of resident control and ownership in self-help housing. *Land Economics* **57**, 106–14.

Carroll, A. 1980. *Pirate subdivisions and the market for residential lots in Bogotá*. City Study Project Paper, no. 7. Washington: The World Bank.
Castells, M. 1977. *The urban question: a marxist approach*. London: Edward Arnold.
Castells, M. 1979. *City, class and power*. London: Macmillan.
Castells, M. 1983. *The city and the grassroots*. London: Edward Arnold.

Chant, S. 1984. *Las olvidadas: a study of women, housing and family structure in Querétaro, Mexico.* Unpublished PhD thesis, University of London.

Cibotti, R. *et al.* 1974. Evolución y perspectivas de los procesos de planificación en América Latina. In *Experiencias y problemas de planificación en América Latina.* Mexico: Siglo Veintiuno Editores.

Cisneros, A. n.d. La colonia El Sol. Mexico, DF: mimeo.

Cleaves, P. 1974. *Bureaucratic politics and administration in Chile.* Berkeley: University of California Press.

Cockcroft, J. D. 1983. *Mexico. Class formation, capital accumulation and the state.* New York: Monthly Review Press.

Collier, D. 1976. *Squatters and oligarchs.* Baltimore: Johns Hopkins University Press.

Collier, D. (ed.) 1979. *The New Authoritarianism in Latin America.* Princeton: Princeton University Press.

Connolly, P. 1981. *Towards an analysis of Mexico City's local state.* Mimeo.

Connolly, P. 1982. Uncontrolled settlements and self-build: what kind of solution? The Mexico City case. In *Self-help housing: a critique,* P. M. Ward (ed.), 141–74. London: Mansell.

Connolly, P. 1984. Finanzas públicas y el estado local: el caso del DDF. *Revista de Ciencias sociales y humanidades – UAM* 5 (11), 57–91.

COPEVI, 1977a. *La producción de vivienda en la zona metropolitana de la ciudad de México.* Mexico DF: COPEVI Asociación Civil.

COPEVI. 1977b. *Investigación sobre vivienda: las políticas habitacionales del estado mexicano.* Mexico DF: COPEVI Asociación Civil.

COPEVI. 1977c. *Análisis del comportamiento del mercado de bienes raices en la zona metropolitana de la ciudad de México.* Mimeo. Mexico DF: COPEVI A.C.

COPEVI. 1978. *Estudio de densidades habitacionales y revisión de la zonificación secundaria.* Mimeo, various volumes. Mexico DF: COPEVI A.C.

Cordera, R. and C. Tello 1983. *México: la disputa por la nación,* 4th edn. Mexico DF: Siglo XXI.

Cornelius, W. 1973. Contemporary Mexico: a structural analysis of urban caciquismo. In *The caciques: oligarchical politics and the system of caciquismo,* R. Kern (ed.), 135–91. Albuquerque: University of New Mexico Press.

Cornelius, W. 1975. *Politics and the migrant poor in Mexico City.* California: Stanford University Press.

Crooke, P. 1983. Popular housing supports and the urban housing market. In *People, poverty and shelter: problems of self-help housing in the Third World,* R. Skinner and M. Rodell (eds), 173–91. London: Methuen.

Cruz Rodriguez, M. n.d. *El ejido en la urbanización de la ciudad de México.* Licenciatura thesis. Mexico DF: UAM, Azcapotzalco.

Cullen, M. and S. Woolery (eds) 1982. *World congress on land policy.* Lexington: Lexington Books.

Da Camargo, C. P. *et al.* 1976. *São Paulo: crescimento e pobreza.* São Paulo: Edicões Loyola.

De la Madrid, M. 1982. *Los grandes retos de la Ciudad de México,* Mexico DF: Grijalbo.

De la Rosa, M. 1974. *Netzahualcóyotl: un fenomeno.* Mexico DF: Testimonios del Fondo.

De Mattos, C. 1979. Plans versus planning in Latin American experience. *CEPAL Review* 8, 75–90.

Devas, N. 1983. Financing urban land development for low income housing. *Third World Planning Review* 5 (3), 209–25.

Diesing, P. 1962. *Reason in society.* Chicago: University of Illinois Press.

Dietz, H. 1977. Land invasion and consolidation: a study of working poor/governmental relations in Lima, Peru. *Urban Anthropology* 6, 371–85.

Dietz, H. 1980. *Poverty and problem solving under military rule: the urban poor in Lima, Peru.* Austin: University of Texas Press.

Dixon, J. (ed.) 1985. *Social welfare in Asia.* London: Croom Helm.

Doebele, W. 1975. *The private market and low income urbanization in developing countries: the 'pirate' subdivision of Bogotá.* Department of City and Regional Planning, Discussions Paper D75–11. Cambridge Mass.: Harvard University.

Doebele, W. 1983. The provision of land for the urban poor: concepts, instruments and prospects. In *Land for housing the poor*, S. Angel *et al*. (eds), 348–74. Singapore: Select Books.

Durand, J. 1983. *La ciudad invade el ejido*. Mexico DF: Ediciones de la Casa Chata.

Durand-Lasserve, A. 1983. The land conversion process in Bangkok and the predominance of the private sector over the public sector. In *Land for housing the poor*, S. Angel *et al*. (eds), 284–309. Singapore: Select Books.

Eckstein, S. 1977. *The poverty of revolution: the state and the urban poor in Mexico*. Princeton NJ: Princeton University Press.

Edwards, M. 1982. Cities of tenants: renting among the urban poor in Latin America. In *Urbanization in contemporary Latin America*, A. G. Gilbert *et al*. (eds), 129–58. Chichester: Wiley.

Elling, R. H. 1981. The fiscal crisis of the state and state financing of health care. *Social Science and Medicine* **15C**, 207–17.

Evers, H. 1976. Urban expansion and land ownership in underdeveloped societies. In *The city in comparative perspective*, J. Walton and L. Masotti (eds), 67–79. Beverly Hills: Sage.

Eyles, J. and K. Woods 1983. *The social geography of medicine and health*. London: Croom Helm.

Fagen, R. and W. Tuohy 1972. *Politics and privilege in a Mexican city*. California: Stanford University Press.

Ferras, R. 1978. *Ciudad Netzahualcóyotl: un barrio en via de absorción por la ciudad de México*. Mexico DF: Centro de Estudios Sociológicos, El Colegio de México.

Fideurbe 1976. *Informe de labores 1973–77*. Mexico DF: Agency publication.

Flores, E. 1958. *Tratada sobre economía agrícola*. Mexico DF: Fondo de Cultura.

Fox, D. 1972. Patterns of morbidity and mortality in Mexico City. *Geographical Review* **62**, 151–86.

Fried, R. 1972. Mexico City. In *Great cities of the world*, W. Robson and D. Regan (eds), 3rd edn, 645–88. Beverly Hills: Sage.

Frieden, W. 1965. The search for a housing policy in Mexico City. *Town Planning Review* **36**, 75–94.

Friedmann, J. 1965. *Venezuela: from doctrine to dialogue*. Syracuse: Syracuse University Press.

Garavita Elias, R. 1983. La protección al salario. *Análisis Económico* **2**, 121–50. Mexico: UAM Azcapotzalco.

García, B., H. Muñoz and O. de Oliveira 1982. *Hogares y trabajadores en la Ciudad de México*. Mexico DF: El Colegio de México and the Instituto de Investigaciones Sociales, UNAM.

Garza, G. 1978. *Ciudad de México: dinámica ecónomica y factores locacionales*. Mexico DF: Temas de la Ciudad, DDF.

Garza, G. and M. Schteingart 1978. *La acción habitacional del estado mexicano*. Mexico DF: El Colegio de México.

Geisse, G. and F. Sabatini 1982. Urban land-market studies in Latin America: issues and methodology. In *World congress on land policy*, M. Cullen and S. Woolery (eds), 149–76. Lexington: Lexington Books.

George, V. and P. Wilding 1975. *Ideology and social welfare*. London: Routledge & Kegan Paul.

Gilbert, A. 1974. *Latin American development: a geographical perspective*. London: Penguin.

Gilbert, A. 1978. Bogotá: politics, planning and the crisis of lost opportunities. In *Latin American urban research*, vol. 6, W. Cornelius and R. Kemper (eds), 87–126. London: Sage.

Gilbert, A. 1981a. Pirates and invaders: land acquisition in urban Colombia and Venezuela. *World Development* **9**, 657–78.

Gilbert, A. 1981b. Bogotá: an analysis of power in an urban setting. In *Urban problems and planning in the modern world*, M. Pacione (ed.), 65–93. London: Croom Helm.

Gilbert, A. 1983. The tenants of self-help housing: choice and constraint in the housing market. *Development and Change* **14**, 449–77.

Gilbert, A. 1984. *Self-help housing and state intervention: illustrated reflections on the petty-commodity production debate*. Paper presented to Colloquium of British–Mexican Geographers, Mexico City, September.

Gilbert, A. and D. Goodman (eds) 1976. *Development planning and spatial structure*. Chichester: Wiley.

Gilbert, A. and J. Gugler 1982. *Cities, poverty and development: urbanization in the Third World*. Oxford: Oxford University Press.

Gilbert, A. and P. Ward 1982. The state and low-income housing. In *Urbanization in contemporary Latin America*, A. Gilbert *et al*. (eds), 79–128. Chichester: Wiley.

Gilbert, A. and P. Ward 1985. *Housing, the state and the poor: policy and practice in three Latin American cities*. Cambridge: Cambridge University Press.

Gilbert, N. and H. Specht 1974. *Dimensions of social welfare policy*. Englewood Cliffs NJ: Prentice Hall.

Glennerster, H. 1975. *Social service budgets and social policy: British and American experience*. London: Allen & Unwin.

González Casanova, P. 1970. *Democracy in Mexico*. New York: Oxford University Press.

Goulet, D. 1983. *Mexico: development strategies for the future*. Notre Dame, Indiana: University of Notre Dame Press.

Grindle. M. 1977. *Bureaucrats, politicians and peasants in Mexico: a case study in public policy*. Berkeley: University of California Press.

Guerrero, M. T. *et al*. 1974. *La tierra, especulación y fraude en el fraccionamiento de San Agustín*. Mexico DF: mimeo.

Haddad, E. 1982. Report on urban land market research in São Paulo, Brazil. In *World congress on land policy*. M. Cullen and S. Wollery (eds), 201–16. Lexington: Lexington Books.

Hansen, R. 1974. *The politics of Mexican development*, 2nd edn. Baltimore: Johns Hopkins University Press.

Hardiman, M. and J. Midgley 1982. *The social dimensions of development: social policy and planning in the Third World*. Chichester: Wiley.

Hardoy, J. and D. Satterthwaite 1981. *Shelter, need and response: housing, land and settlement policies in 17 Third World nations*. Chichester: Wiley.

Harloe, M. 1977. *Captive cities*. Chichester: John Wiley.

Harth, J. A. and M. Silva 1982. Mutual help and progressive development housing: for what purpose? *Self-help housing: a critique*, P. M. Ward (ed.), 233–50. London: Mansell.

Heath, J. 1985. Contradictions in Mexican food policy. *Politics in Mexico*, G. Philip (ed.), London: Croom Helm.

Huntingdon, S. P. 1968. *Political order in changing societies*. New Haven: Yale University Press.

IDS (Institute of Development Studies) 1981. *Organizing for health*. Sussex: Development Research Digest.

Iglesias, E. V. 1984. La evolución económica de América Latina en 1983. *Comercio Exterior* 34, 185–200.

IMF (International Monetary Fund) 1984. *International financial statistics*. Washington: IMF.

Iracheta, A. (ed.) 1984. *El suelo, recurso estratégico para el desarrollo urbano*. Toluca: Universidad Autónoma del Estado de México.

Kaplan, M. 1972. *Aspectos políticos de la planificación en América Latina*. Montevideo: Biblioteca Científica.

Kemper, R. 1973. Migration and adaptation of Tzintzuntzán peasants in Mexico City. Unpublished PhD thesis, University of California, Berkeley.

Kowarick, L. 1975. *Capitalismo e marginalidade na América Latina*. Rio de Janeiro: Paz e Terra.

Kusnetzoff, F. 1975. Housing policies or housing politics: an evaluation of the Chilean experience. *Journal of Interamerican Studies and World Affairs* 17, 291–310.

Lea, J. 1983. Customary land tenure and urban housing land: partnership and participation in developing societies. In *Land for housing the poor*, S. Angel *et al.* (eds), 54–74. Singapore: Select Books.

Leeds, A. 1969. The significant variables determining the character of squatter settlements. *América Latina* 12, 44–86.

Leeds, A. and E. Leeds 1976. Accounting for behavioural differences: three political systems and responses of squatters in Brazil, Peru, and Chile. In *The city in comparative perspective*, J. Walton and L. Masotti (eds), 193–248. Beverly Hills: Sage.

Legoretta, J. 1983. El acceso a la tierra urbana y el mercado inmobiliario popular, socieded Interamericana de Planificación, *Relación campo-ciudad: la tierra, recurso estrategica para el desarrollo y la transformación social*. Mexico DF: Ediciones SIAP, 417–42.

Linn, J. F. 1983. *Cities in the developing world: policies for their equitable and efficient growth*. Oxford: Oxford University Press.

Lojkine, J. 1976. Contribution to a Marxist theory of capitalist urbanization. In *Urban sociology: critical essays*, C. Pickvance (ed.), 119–46. London: Tavistock.

Lomnitz, L. 1977. *Networks and marginality*. New York: Academic Press.

López Acuña, D. 1980. *La salud desigual en México*. Mexico DF: Siglo XXI.

López Díaz, C. 1978. *La intervención del estado en la formación de un asentamiento proletario: el caso de la colonia Ajusco*. Licenciatura thesis, Department of Anthropology, Universidad Iberoamericana, Mexico DF.

Lozano, E. 1975. Housing and the urban poor in Chile: contrasting experiences under 'Christian Democracy' and 'Unidad Popular'. In *Latin American urban research*, vol. 5, W. Cornelius and F. Trueblood (eds), 177–96. London: Sage.

Mabogunje, A. L., J. E. Hardoy and R. P. Misra 1978. *Shelter provision in developing countries*. New York: Wiley.

McCullum, J. 1974. Land values in Bogotá, Colombia. *Land Economics* 50, 312–17.

Makin, J. 1984. *Self-help housing in Mexico City, and the role of the state*. Unpublished PhD thesis, Heriot Watt University.

Malloy, J. 1979. *The politics of social security in Brazil*. Pittsburgh: University of Pittsburgh Press.

Malloy, J. and S. Borzutzky 1982. Politics, social welfare policy and the population problem in Latin America. *International Journal of Health Services* 12, 77–98.

Martin, R. 1983. Upgrading *People, poverty and shelter*, R. Skinner and M. Rodell (eds), 53–79. London: Methuen.

Mesa Lago, C. 1978. *Social security in Latin America: pressure groups, stratification and inequality*. Pittsburgh: University of Pittsburgh Press.

Mexico, BNH (Banco Nacional Hipotecario). 1952. *El problema dela habitación en la Ciudad de México*. Mexico DF: BNH report.

Mexico, COPLAMAR 1982. *Necesidades esenciales en México: Salud*. Mexico DF: Siglo XXI.

Mexico, DDF (Departmento de Distrito Federal) 1976. *Plan Director*. Mexico DF: DDF publication.

Mexico, DDF 1979. Ley Organica del DF. In *DDF Impuestos del Departamento del Distrito Federal*. DF: Ediciones.

Mexico, DDF 1980. *Plan de desarrollo urbano: plan general del Plan Director. Versión abreviada*. Mexico DF: DDF publication.

Mexico, DDF. 1982. *Sistema de planificación urbana del Distrite Federal*. Mexico DF: DDF publication.

Mexico, INVI (Instituto Nacional de Vivienda) 1958. *Las colonias populares de la Ciudad de México: problemas y soluciones*. Mexico DF: INVI publication.

Mexico, SAHOP 1978. *Plan nacional de desarrollo urbano. Versión abreviada*. Mexico DF: Agency publication.

Mexico, SAHOP 1979. *La incorporación de los procesos que generan los asentamientos irregulares a la planeación de los centros de población*. Mexico DF: SAHOP, DGCP.

Mexico, SPP 1983a. *El sistema nacional de planeación democrática*. Mexico DF: SPP publication.

Mexico, SPP. 1983b. *Plan nacional de desarrollo, 1983–88*. Mexico DF: SPP publication.

Midgley, J. 1984. *Social security, inequality and the Third World*. Chichester,: Wiley.

Miliband, R. 1969. *The state in capitalist society*. London: Weidenfeld & Nicolson.

Miliband, R. 1977. *Marxism and politics*. Oxford: Oxford University Press.

Mohan, R. and R. Villamizar 1982. The evolution of land values in the context of rapid urban growth: a case study of Bogotá and Cali, Colombia. In *World congress on land policy*, M. Cullen and S. Woolery (eds), 217–54. Lexington: Lexington Books.

Montaño, J. 1976. *Los pobres de le ciudad de México en los asentamientos espontáneos*. Mexico DF: Siglo XXI.

Moreno Toscano, A. 1979. La 'crisis' en la ciudad. In *Mexico hoy*, P. González Casanova and E. Florescano (eds), 152–76. Mexico DF: Siglo XXI.

Moser, C. 1982. A home of one's own: squatter housing strategies in Guayaquil, Ecuador. In *Urbanization in contemporary Latin America*, A. Gilbert *et al.* (eds), 159–90. Chichester: Wiley.

Muñoz, H., O. Oliviera and C. Stern (eds) 1977. *Migracíon y marginalidad ocupacional*. Mexico DF: Universidad Nacional Autónoma de México.

Nalvern, J. 1978. *The politics of urban growth: a case study of community formation in Calí, Colombia*. Unpublished PhD thesis, University of California, San Diego.

Navarette, I. Martínez de. 1970. La distribución del ingreso en México: tendencias y perspectivas. In *El perfil de México en 1980*, vol 1, D. Ibarra *et al.* (eds), 15–71. Mexico DF: Siglo XXI.

Navarro, V. 1974. The underdevelopment of health or the health of underdevelopment: an analysis of the distribution of human health resources in Latin America. *International Journal of Health Services* 4 (1), 5–27.

Navarro, V. 1978. *Class struggle, the state and medicine*. New York: Martin Robertson.

Needler, M. 1982. *Mexican politics: the containment of conflict*. New York: Praeger.

Nelson, J. 1979. *Access to power: politics and the urban poor in developing nations*. Princeton NJ: Princeton University Press.

Nuñez, O. 1983. Causas sociales y políticas en las mobvilizaciones de los colonos en el DF, 1970–73. *Tabique* 2, 3–33.

O'Connor, J. 1973. *The fiscal crisis of the state*. New York: St Martin's Press.

O'Donnell, G. 1973. *Modernization and bureaucratic authoritarianism: studies in South American politics*. Berkeley: University of California Press.

O'Donnell, G. 1974. Corporatism and the question of the state. In *Authoritarianism and corporatism in Latin America*, J. Malloy (ed.), 47–87. Pittsburgh: University of Pittsburgh Press.

Padgett, L. V. 1966. *The Mexican political system*. Boston: Houghton Mifflin.

Padilla Aragón, E. 1981. *México: hacia el crecimiento con distribución del ingreso*. Mexico DF: Siglo XXI.

Pahl, R. 1975. *Whose city?* Harmondsworth: Penguin.

Payne, G. (ed.) 1984. *Low-income housing in the developing world*. Chichester: Wiley.

Peattie, L. 1979. Housing policy in developing countries: two puzzles. *World Development* 7, 1017–22.

Perló, M. 1979. Política y vivienda en México, 1910–1952. *Revista Mexicana de Sociología* 3, 769–835.

Perló, M. 1980. Los problemas financieros de la Cd. de México. *El Día*, 7 June 1984.

Perló, M. 1981. *Estado, vivienda y estructura urbana en el Cardenismo*. Mexico DF: UNAM, Cuadernos de investigación social 3, Instituto de Investigaciones Sociales.

Perló, M. n.d. *De como perdió la Cd. de México su municipalidad sin obtener un cambio ni una democracía de manzana*. Mexico DF: mimeo.

Pommier, P. 1982. The place of Mexico City in the nation's growth: employment trends and policies. *International Labour Review* 121, 345–60.

Portes, A. 1979. Housing policy, urban poverty, and the state: the favelas of Rio de Janeiro, 1972–76. Latin American Research Review 14, 3–24.

Poulantzas, N. 1973. *Political power and social classes*. London: New Left Books.

Pradilla, E. 1976. Notas acerca del 'problem de vivienda'. *Ideología y Sociedad* 16, 70–107.

Purcell, S. and J. Purcell 1980. State and society in Mexico. *World Politics* 32, 194–227.

Ray, T. 1969. *The politics of the barrio*. Berkeley: University of California Press.

Rivera Ortiz, A. I. 1976. *The politics of development planning in Colombia*. Unpublished PhD thesis, State University of New York at Buffalo.

Roberts, B. 1978. *Cities of peasants: the political economy of urbanization in the Third World*. London: Edward Arnold.

Rodgers, W. D. 1967. *The twilight struggle: the Alliance for Progress and the politics of development in Latin America*. New York: Random House.

Rodríguez Araujo, O. 1979: *La reforma política y los partidos en México*. Mexico DF: Siglo XXI.

Rodwin, L. et al. 1969. *Planning urban growth and regional development*. Cambridge Mass.: MIT Press.

Roxborough, I. 1984. *Unions and politics in Mexico: the case of the auto industry*. Cambridge: Cambridge University Press.

Saldivar, A. 1981. *Ideología y política del estado mexicano 1970–76*, 2nd ed. Mexico DF: Siglo XXI.

Saunders, P. 1979. *Urban politics: a sociological interpretation*. Harmondsworth: Penguin.

Schers, D. 1972. *The popular sector of the PRI in Mexico*. Unpublished PhD thesis, University of New Mexico.

Schteingart, M. 1981. Formación y consolidación de un asentamiento popular en México: el caso de ciudad Netzahualcóyotl. *Revista Interamericana de Planificación* 57, 100–14.

Scott, I. 1982. *Urban and spatial development in Mexico*. Baltimore: Johns Hopkins University Press.

Scott, R. 1964. *Mexican government in transition*. Illinois: University of Illinois Press.

Seminario de Estudios Urbanos (SEU). 1984. *Política urbana en el primer año de Gobierno de Miguel de la Madrid*. Mexico DF: mimeo.

Shroup, D. 1978. Land taxation and government participation in urban land markets. In *Urban land policy issues and opportunities*, H. Dunkerley (ed). Washington: World Bank Special Working Paper No. 283.

Skinner, R. 1983. Community participation: its scope and organization. In *People, poverty and shelter: problems of self-help housing in the Third World*, R. Skinner and M. Rodell (eds), 125–50. London: Methuen.

Smith, P. 1979. *Labyrinths of power: political recruitment in twentieth century Mexico*. Princeton NJ: Princeton University Press.

Soberón, J. and J. Narro. 1984. *El programa de salud para los grandes urbes en México*. Mexico DF: mimeo SSA.

Stohr, W. 1972. *El desarrollo regional en América Latina. Experiencias y perspectivas*. Buenos Aires: Ediciones SIAP.

Sudra, T. 1976. *Low-income housing system in Mexico City*. Unpublished PhD thesis, MIT.

Tello, C. 1978. *La política económica en México, 1970–1976*. Mexico DF: Siglo XXI.

Terrazas, O. and L. Flores 1978. *La producción de vivienda en Ixtacalco zona expropriada*. Licenciatura thesis, National School of Architecture, UNAM.

Turnbull, S. 1983. Cooperative land banks for low-income housing. In *Land for housing the poor*, S. Angel et al. (eds), 512–27. Singapore: Select Books.

Turner, J. F. C. 1968. Housing priorities, settlement patterns and urban development in modernizing countries. *Journal of the American Institute of Planners* 34, 354–63.

Turner, J. F. C. 1969. Uncontrolled urban settlements: problems and policies. In *The city in newly developing countries*, G. Breese (ed.), 507–31. Englewood Cliffs NJ: Prentice Hall.

Turner, J. F. C. 1976. *Housing by people*. London: Marion Boyars.

Ugalde, A., L. Olson, D. Schers and M. Von Hoegen 1974. *The urbanization process of a poor Mexican neighbourhood: the case of San Felipe del Real Adicional, Juárez*. Austin: Institute of Latin American Studies, University of Texas.

Unikel, L. 1972. *La dinámica del crecimiento de la Ciudad de México*. Mexico DF: Fundación para estudios de población.

Unikel, L. and A. Lavell 1979. El problema urbano en México. Mimeo.

United Nations: ECLA 1970. Popular participation in development. In *Social Change and social development policy*. New York: United Nations.

United Nations 1980. *Yearbook of national accounts statistics*. New York: United Nations.

Valladares, L. 1978. Working the system: squatter response to resettlement in Rio de Janeiro. *International Journal of Urban and Regional Research* 2, 12–25.

Varley, A. 1985. 'Ya somos dueños'. *Ejido land regularization and development in Mexico City*. Unpublished PhD thesis, University of London.

Vernez, G. 1973. *The residential movements of low-income families: the case of Bogotá, Colombia*. New York: Rand Institute.

Villamizar, R. 1980. *Land prices in Bogotá between 1955 and 1978: a descriptive analysis*. World Bank City Project Paper, no. 10. Washington: World Bank.

Ward, P. 1976a. The squatter settlement as slum or housing solution: the evidence from Mexico City. *Land Economics* 52, 330–46.

Ward, P. 1976b. *In search of a home: social and economic characteristics of squatter settlements and the role of self-help housing in Mexico City*. Unpublished PhD thesis, University of Liverpool.

Ward, P. 1981a. Political pressure for urban services: the response of two Mexico City administrations. *Development and Change* 12, 379–407.

Ward, P. 1981b. Mexico City. In *Urban problems and planning in Third World cities*, M. Pacione (ed.), 28–64. London: Croom Helm.

Ward, P. 1981c. Financing land acquisition for self-build housing schemes. *Third World Planning Review* 3, 7–20.

Ward, P. 1982a. Informal housing: conventional wisdoms reappraised. *Built Environment* 8, 85–94.

Ward, P. 1982b. The practice and potential of self-help housing in Mexico City. In *Self-help housing: a critique*, P. M. Ward (ed.), 175–208. London: Mansell.

Ward, P. (ed.) 1982c. *Self-help housing: a critique*. London: Mansell.

Ward, P. 1983. Land for housing the poor: what can planners contribute? In *Land for housing the poor*, S. Angel *et al.* (eds), 34–53. Singapore: Select Books.

Weisskoff, R. and A. Figueroa 1976. Traversing the social pyramid: a comparative review of income distribution in Latin America. *Latin American Research Review* 2, 71–112.

Wells, J. 1983. Industrial accumulation and living standards in the long-run: the São Paulo industrial working class 1930–75, Parts I and II. *Journal of Development Studies*, 19, nos. 1 and 2.

Whitehead, L. 1980. Mexico from bust to boom: a political evaluation of the 1976–9 stabilization program. *World Development* 8, 843–63.

Whitehead, L. 1981. On 'governability' in Mexico. *Bulletin of Latin Am. Research* 1, 27–47.

Whitehead, L. 1984. *Politics of economic management*. Seminar given in 'Mexico 1984' conference held at the Institute of Latin American Studies, London, 4–5 June.

World Bank 1972. *Urbanization*. Sector Policy Paper. Washington: World Bank.

World Bank 1980a. *Shelter*. Washington: World Bank.

World Bank 1980b. *Water supply and waste disposal*. Poverty and Basic Needs series. Washington: World Bank.

World Bank 1984. *World development report*. Washington: World Bank.

Wynia, G. 1972. *Politics and planners: economic development policy in Central America*. Madison, Wisconsin: University of Wisconsin Press.

Author index

Subject index

Numbers in italics refer to text figures.